yǎn　　zhōng　　xué
演　中　学

Setting the Stage for CHINESE

Plays and Performances for Grades K-6

By Yuanchao Meng
孟援朝

CHENG & TSUI COMPANY
Boston

Copyright © 2008 by Yuanchao Meng

All rights reserved. No part of this publication may be reproduced or transmitted in any form or by any means, electronic or mechanical, including photocopying, recording, scanning, or any information storage or retrieval system, without written permission from the publisher.

17 16 15 14 13 12 11 10 09 08   1 2 3 4 5 6 7 8 9 10

Published by
Cheng & Tsui Company, Inc.
25 West Street
Boston, MA 02111-1213 USA
Fax (617) 426-3669
www.cheng-tsui.com
"Bringing Asia to the World"™

ISBN: 978-0-88727-529-6

Library of Congress Cataloging-in-Publication Data
Meng, Yuanchao.
    Setting the stage for Chinese : plays & performances for grades K-6 / Yuanchao Meng
= Yan zhong xue : [chu ji ben / Meng Yuanchao]
        p. cm.
    In English and Chinese.
    Parallel title in pinyin and Chinese characters.
    ISBN 978-0-88727-529-6
  1. Chinese language--Textbooks for foreign speakers--English. 2. Chinese language--Study and teaching--English. I. Title. II. Title: Yan zhong xue.

PL1129.E5M46 2007
372.65'951--dc22
                                                2007062005

Illustrated by 雁雏

Printed in Canada

Publisher's Note

The Cheng & Tsui Chinese Language Series is designed to publish and widely distribute quality language learning materials created by leading instructors from around the world. We welcome readers' comments and suggestions concerning the publications in this series. Please contact the following members of our Editorial Board, in care of our Editorial Department (e-mail: editor@cheng-tsui.com).

Professor Shou-hsin Teng, Chief Editor
Graduate Institute of Teaching Chinese as a Second Language
National Taiwan Normal University

Professor Dana Scott Bourgerie
Department of Asian and Near Eastern Languages
Brigham Young University

Professor Samuel Cheung
Department of Chinese
Chinese University of Hong Kong

Professor Ying-che Li
Department of East Asian Languages and Literatures
University of Hawaii

Professor Timothy Light
Department of Comparative Religion
Western Michigan University

About the Author

Yuanchao Meng teaches Chinese in the Newton Public School System in Newton, Massachusetts, where she has been performing the plays in this book with her students for over ten years. Her Master's Degree in Education is from Bridgewater State College in Bridgewater, Massachusetts.

CONTENTS
内 容 目 录

Preface	vii
Acknowledgments	xi

1. **Happy Chinese New Year** *(A Holiday Rhyme)*
   过 年 好
   Play 1
   Teaching Reference 6

2. **The Ants and the Grasshopper** *(A Total Physical Response [TPR] Story)*
   蚂 蚁 和 蚱 蜢
   Play 9
   Teaching Reference 20

3. **The Little Tadpoles Look for Their Mother** *(A Fairy Tale Skit)*
   小 蝌 蚪 找 妈 妈
   Play 23
   Teaching Reference 36

4. **The Turtle and the Hare** *(Adapted from Aesop's Fables)*
   龟 兔 赛 跑
   Play 39
   Teaching Reference 52

5. **The Legend of Mulan** *(A Chinese Legend)*
   木 兰 的 传 说
   Play 55
   Teaching Reference 62

6. **The Turnip Is Back** *(A Fairy Tale Skit)*
   萝卜回来了

   Play 65

   Teaching Reference 92

7. **Mimi Says** *(A TPR Class Activity)* 95
   咪咪说（课堂活动）

   Teaching Reference 102

8. **Me** *(A TPR Class Activity)* 105
   我（课堂活动）

   Teaching Reference 108

PREFACE

Setting the Stage for Chinese was drafted ten years ago when I began to teach Chinese at elementary schools in Newton, Massachusetts. Since then I have continuously revised the plays as I teach them, and the end result is this current volume.

Setting the Stage for Chinese is designed to reinforce basic communication skills in Chinese at the elementary level. When students finish performing any of the plays in this book, they will feel proud to have completed a successful presentation in Chinese in front of an audience of classmates, parents, and teachers.

The six plays in this volume draw upon well-known fables, as well as traditional Chinese legends and fairy tales. Stories such as Aesop's famous "The Turtle and the Hare," and China's "The Legend of Mulan" and "The Turnip Is Back," are re-created in the form of rhymes, short plays, and poems suitable for performing on stage.

Children love to perform, and much language learning takes place during the preparation of a dramatic performance. While reading the plays, students build reading skills and learn new words. While practicing their roles, they learn correct pronunciation, intonation, and rhythm. While performing, they gain confidence to speak in a foreign language in front of an audience. Throughout the learning process, they are having fun and learning a new language and culture. While textbook instruction is clearly necessary, my goal is to make Chinese learning more lively, interesting, and fun. To enrich language learning and to make it enjoyable, threads of Chinese culture are woven into the plays.

The scripts in this book can be used to present a stage production and can also be adapted for short recitations and speaking practice in class. Your imagination and creativity will add color to the original stories. Hints and suggestions for performance are contained between the lines of each script in parentheses with italics.

Special Features

   a. The plays are student-centered, and can be used for either classroom practice or full-length performance.
   b. The material can be adapted by teachers of Chinese in both heritage and mainstream schools, according to their curriculum requirements and students' needs.

c. A Teaching Reference page in Chinese and English follows each play and contains background information, teaching suggestions, preparatory steps for teaching and performing the plays, and assessment guidelines.

d. The plays are written in simple and easy-to-understand Chinese, suitable for children in grades K-6 or at a beginning level of Chinese language proficiency.

e. The plays are written in both Chinese and English, with pinyin included to help students pronounce words correctly.

f. At the end of the book, there are two fun and useful classroom activities, "Mimi Says" and "Me," that will help get students warmed up to performance and oral recitation.

Suggestions for Getting Started

a. Plan well and start early. For example, if you want to produce a Spring Festival celebration, you should match students with their roles before the holiday season begins.

b. Leave a few minutes each day for students to review their parts while keeping regular curriculum routines. Go over the roles from time to time and make corrections when necessary. By practicing new vocabulary for a short time each day, students will have an easier time remembering new words.

c. Encourage teamwork. Make sure that every student has a part to play and every student contributes.

d. Performances can take place on stage in an auditorium, at the school cafeteria, or in a classroom.

As I have taught these plays over the years, many of my students have come back to me and recited some of the lines they learned. They tell me that they forgot many of the things they learned in their textbooks, but never forgot the words to the stories and rhymes they learned in my class.

I hope you have fun reading the scripts and performing these plays. To view photos of stage props and costumes, read more teaching suggestions, and share your own ideas with other teachers, please visit the *Setting the Stage for Chinese* web site at **www.cheng-tsui.com**.

Yuanchao Meng

May 2007

前 言

一、这本书的内容

"演中学"这本书的草稿是十年前我在牛顿小学教中文时写的，后来一直给学生用，一直不断修改，又增添了些内容就成了现在这本书。小品和歌谣都是学生们在春节联欢晚会上表演过的节目，也能在一个学年里不同的时间选用。

书中的六个故事，是从大家熟悉的寓言、传说和童话故事中选出，例如"龟兔赛跑"、"木兰的故事"和"萝卜回来了"等。这些故事被重新改编成人物对话形式的童谣、小品、短剧或带动说唱，适合舞台表演。

孩子们好动，喜欢表演，语言的学习大部分发生在他们准备表演节目的过程中。读剧本的时候，他们能提高阅读能力，学新词汇；排练的时候，他们主动纠正自己的语音和语调；站在观众面前表演的时候，他们对说中文增添了自信心。在整个学演的过程中，孩子们兴致勃勃，跃跃欲试。按照教科书的教学固然非常重要，然而我的目标是让孩子们学得更生动活泼，更有乐趣。为丰富语言教学，增加趣味，文化的点滴贯穿在小品中。

书中的内容可以做舞台表演的剧本，也可以做课堂上朗诵和阅读的材料。您的想象和再创造可以为这些故事添加色彩。一些表演中的建议和暗示我用斜体字括弧在字里行间，仅供参考。

二、教材的特点

教材以学生为中心，可以直接在课堂上使用，节省教师备课时间。所选内容在学生练习掌握后，可以直接在春节晚会或汇报演出上使用，有助教师编排准备，事半功倍。

教师可以方便地利用教材来调节教学教程的节奏。书中故事小品角色有轻有重，适合学生的不同程度，可为汉语水平不齐的一班学生找到更多尝试、发挥和表现的机会。

在每个小品的后面有中英对照的教师参考，包括故事背景介绍、教学建议、准备步骤和评估小结。

教材力求叙述语言简短，诗歌琅琅上口，学生乐于背诵，有助提高学生语音语调的掌握。

教材中语言词汇有英文对照，有助学生理解和自学。汉字上面有拼音有助学生的正确发音。

书的最后还有两个课堂活动内容，趣味性高，可以灵活使用，帮助学生掌握小品中的词汇。

三、教材的使用

周全计划，早做准备。如果想春节前后开联欢会，大约在新年前一个月要把材料选好发给学生，让学生挑选好角色。平常的教学课程照常，但每天要留五到十分钟的时间让学生熟悉各自的角色。要及时纠正学生的语音语调。

鼓励合作，各尽所能。班上每个人都要为演出担任一个角色。人物角色不够可选两个故事同时进行。不要太顾虑学生的词汇还没有达到故事内容的程度，循序渐进中的跳跃，可以给课堂增添生气，使学生们有目的地加倍努力。

灵活掌握汇报演出的场地，学校礼堂，餐厅或是普通教室都可以使用。

这本书是为加强基础汉语交流沟通而设计的。当学生们读过书中的任何一个小品并能在同学、家长和老师们面前表演时，他们会感到非常自豪。高中学生回来看我，还会背诵他们在小学时学的中文歌谣。有的说，她们课本上的内容忘了不少，可仍记得她们小品中的的台词。

希望您有兴趣阅读这些小品并把它们搬上舞台。有关舞台道具，服装设计方面更具体的建议，请上网 www.cheng-tsui.com 在演中学的网址上查寻，并请留下您的宝贵意见。

孟援朝
二零零七年五月

Acknowledgments

Setting the Stage for Chinese is based on famous fables known to children around the world, as well as Chinese fairy tales, legends, and mythology, which have been around for generations. These timeless stories were part of my childhood, and this book honors the original stories, which inspired me and influenced my thinking.

During the long writing process, I am very grateful to Mr. Robert Leary, who had the patience to read the earliest versions of the plays contained in this book. He spent an enormous amount time polishing the English portions while sharing his insight from the viewpoint of a Westerner. His detailed critique has been very helpful.

I am also very grateful to Professor Ye Leili at the University of Massachusetts, Boston. She inspired me, encouraged me, and dedicated generous amounts of her time to go over the stories and share her valuable thoughts with me.

I extend my thanks to the Newton Public School System, especially to Jody Klein, who has supported me in many ways and promoted the Chinese program over the past nine years. My thanks also go to Carolyn Henderson and Charlotte Manson, who secured a grant for the Chinese program from the Freeman Foundation from 2001–2004. The grant made it possible for me to work on these performances as extracurricular activities for my students.

I am extremely grateful to Oak Hill Middle School, PTO, and the parents of the community. They have supported the Chinese evening program for the past six years. Many thanks go to the wonderful students from Oak Hill Middle School, Brown Middle School, and Memorial-Spaulding School. The students' enthusiasm in learning the stories and their excellent performance keep me going and constantly remind me why I embraced this project in the first place.

My very special thanks go to CLASS (the National Chinese Language Association of Secondary-Elementary Schools). The organization offered me the opportunity to participate in the CLASS 2002 Summer Abroad Program and has been providing me support in the professional community.

Finally, my thanks go to Jill Cheng, President of Cheng & Tsui Company, and Kristen Wanner, Editor. Their assistance and suggestions have made a positive impact on the final draft.

HAPPY CHINESE NEW YEAR

guò nián hǎo
过 年 好

xiǎo péng you men guò nián hǎo
小朋友们，过年好！
Happy New Year, little friends! *(students walk onto the stage)*

bà ba mā ma guò nián hǎo
爸爸妈妈过年好！
Happy New Year, Dad and Mom! *(wave hands to parents)*

yé ye nǎi nai guò nián hǎo
爷爷奶奶过年好！
Happy New Year, Grandpa and Grandma! *(bow)*

lǎo shī men guò nián hǎo
老师们过年好！
Happy New Year, teachers! *(salute teachers)*

tóng xué men guò nián hǎo
同学们过年好！
Happy New Year, classmates! *(wave to classmates)*

guò nián hǎo
过 年 好！
Happy Chinese New Year!

xīn nián hǎo xīn nián dào
新 年 好，新 年 到。
Happy New Year, the new year is here.

xiǎo péng you men fàng biān pào
小 朋 友 们 放 鞭 炮。
Children light firecrackers. *(students hold up clusters of paper fireworks)*

pī lǐ pā la pī lǐ pā la fàng biān pào
劈 里 啪 啦 劈 里 啪 啦 放 鞭 炮。
Pop, Pop! The firecrackers are crackling and exploding. *(cover ears with hands)*

xīn nián hǎo xīn nián dào
新 年 好，新 年 到。
Happy New Year, the new year is here.

xiǎo péng you men hā hā xiào
小 朋 友 们 哈 哈 笑。
Children are laughing merrily.

sòng zǒu gǒu nián zhū nián dào
送 走 (狗) 年 (猪) 年 到。
See off the Year of the (Dog); the Year of the (Pig) has arrived.

xīn nián hǎo xīn nián dào
新 年 好，新 年 到。
Happy New Year, the new year is here.

jiā jiā hù hù máng dǎ sǎo
家 家 户 户 忙 打 扫，
Every family is busy cleaning their house,

2 • Setting the Stage

tiē chūn lián pàn fú dào
贴 春 联 盼 福 到。

and putting up good luck signs everywhere. *(two students show a couplet)*

xīn nián hǎo xīn nián dào
新 年 好, 新 年 到。

Happy New Year, the new year is here.

xiǎo péng you men chuān xīn ǎo
小 朋 友 们 穿 新 袄,

Children wear new outfits, *(look at each other's new clothes)*

chī jiǎo zi chī nián gāo
吃 饺 子 吃 年 糕。

and eat dumplings and New Year's cakes. *(hold a plate of dumplings and a sticky rice cake made out of paper)*

(children pretend to eat dumplings and sticky rice cakes; to make the audience laugh, they turn the plates upside down and the paper dumplings and rice cakes "stick to" the plates— do this by connecting paper dumplings and rice cakes to the plates with string)

xīn nián hǎo xīn nián dào
新 年 好, 新 年 到。

Happy New Year, the new year is here.

yé ye nǎi nai gěi hóng bāo
爷 爷 奶 奶 给 红 包,

Grandpa and Grandma give red envelopes,

jū gōng bài nián hǎo rè nào
鞠 躬 拜 年 好 热 闹。

and children bow to show their thanks. *(bow to audience)*

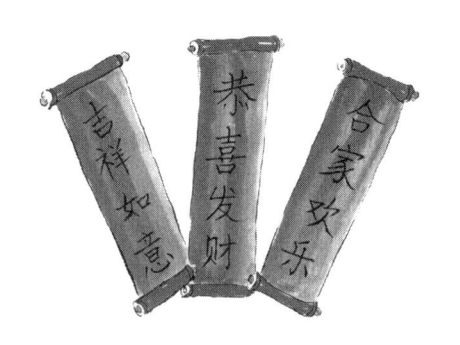

Happy Chinese New Year • 3

xīn nián hǎo xīn nián dào
新年好，新年到。
Happy New Year, the new year is here.

nán nǚ lǎo shào xìng zhì gāo
男女老少兴致高。
People old and young are in high spirits.

gōng xǐ fā cái guò nián hǎo
恭喜发财过年好！
Be happy and prosperous in the new year! *(repeat the last line at a slower tempo)*

THE END

教学参考

背景介绍

中国的新年(春节)是中国和居住在世界各地的中国人最重要的传统节日。这个童谣"过年好",想从小朋友们的眼睛里来反映过年的风俗和乐趣。学生们不但从歌谣中学到如何用中文表达过年时的情景,也能了解过年时人们常做的几件事。

一、放鞭炮是为了辞旧迎新,表示新的一年已经开始。
二、过年以前大扫除是为了不要在过年的日子里把好运扫地出门。
三、门上贴红红的对联最早的原因是为了避邪。现代人是为辞旧迎新。门上贴"倒"着的"福"字是为盼望"福"快些"到"来。
四、吃"年糕"是盼望家人团结,盼望家人总是"黏"在一起。
五、红包是长辈给小辈的压岁钱;小辈要鞠躬(旧时以磕头)表谢意。
六、过年全家要吃年夜饭,拜年从大年初一开始延续两周,亲朋好友之间互访并祝愿彼此万事如意。最常说的是:"恭喜发财、过年好"。

教学建议

这个歌谣适用于小学各个年级,通过表演他们能学到过年时用的词汇,也对中文的童谣有个初步的印象。"过年好"和"新年到"两句台词会重复六遍,可以让大家一起说。表达春节气氛的十二个短句可以分配给十二个学生,一人一句地背诵;也可以根据班上学生人数的多少派对或由小组来完成。教这个童谣大约需要两个课时,教师有节奏地朗读示范很重要。要给学生们一周的时间消化掌握歌谣的内容,利用课前课后的三分钟就能把歌谣过两遍。学生们对自己的台词记得很快,也从反复聆听其他同学的台词中受益。

教学步骤

一、搜集有关中国新年的材料和图片并与全班学生分享。
二、从与搜集材料有关的词汇入手,把童谣中的词汇逐个介绍给学生。
三、学生挑选或是教师指派歌谣中的一段试读。
四、教师帮助学生掌握童谣的节奏,语音和语调。
五、固定适合朗诵童谣各段的学生(个人或小组)。
六、教师检查学生的朗诵并着手制作道具。

舞台表演

按照童谣的脚本,演员一个一个地(或一组一组地)走到台前朗诵。表演没有固定的要求,如观众需要,可先用英语,再用中文。可以用鞭炮、属性的动物、福字、红包等做道具,由演员分别拿着上场。表演时,话不要说得太快,声音要洪亮。即兴的表演更有趣,例如:给观众鞠躬和拱手拜年等。

评估小结

一、学生是否会说童谣的全部或是部分?
二、学生能列举童谣中哪些中国新年的民间风俗?
三、学生还知道或看到过哪些中国新年的活动?(如舞龙、舞狮等)。

请上网 www.cheng-tsui.com 查看作者有关道具制作和选用服装的建议。也请您与大家分享您的好主意和成果。

Teaching Reference

Background Information

Chinese New Year (or Chinese Spring Festival) is the most important holiday for Chinese people living in China and all over the world. The traditions of Chinese New Year are reflected in this children's rhyme. Students learn expressions related to the Chinese New Year and explore some holiday traditions.

1. Fireworks are lit to eliminate bad luck left over from the previous year and to welcome the new year with a "bang."
2. Prior to New Year's Day, Chinese people give their homes a thorough cleaning. They avoid cleaning during the days of Chinese New Year, for fear that good luck might be swept away.
3. In preparation for the New Year's celebration, Chinese people put up red couplets and signs inside and outside their homes, on both sides of their doors or on gateposts. The signs originally were intended to prevent bad luck. Now they are used to help encourage good luck in the coming year.
4. Sticky rice cakes are consumed to reflect a wish that family members unite and stick together in the coming new year.
5. On New Year's Day, the elder members of a family often give the children red envelopes containing money, and the children bow to show their thanks.
6. Chinese New Year celebrations begin with a big family meal on the eve of the lunar new year, and continue for a period of two weeks. Families and friends visit each other and wish each other a happy, prosperous new year.

Teaching Suggestions

This children's rhyme can be used in all elementary grades. Students learn the expressions for Chinese New Year and develop a sense of what Chinese nursery rhymes sound like. Two greeting phrases are repeated six times throughout the rhyme and can be recited by everyone on stage. Twelve different phrases that express the atmosphere of Chinese New Year can be assigned to twelve people. If there are more than twelve people in a class, students can double up and split the the assignment between them.

It will take two class hours to teach the students the rhyme. Teacher should demonstrate how to recite the rhyme many times before students start to try. For a homework assignment, ask students to memorize their own lines; allow one week's time for students to practice every night at home. By the end of the week, students should be able to recite the rhyme together as a class. Spend a couple of minutes each day going over the rhyme during class. Students will pick up the vocabulary quickly and benefit by hearing other student's lines over and over again.

Preparatory Steps

1. Let students collect Chinese New Year materials and pictures and share them with the whole class.
2. Start with easier vocabulary and introduce each phrase in the rhyme one by one.
3. Assign each student one verse of the rhyme to try reciting, or let each student choose one verse.
4. Coach students to say the rhyme with good pronunciation, intonation, and rhythm.
5. Assign each verse to an individual or small group to perform.
6. Prepare the props while checking individuals' or pairs' work.

Stage Performance

With assigned props, students should walk to the front of the stage one by one (or group by group) to recite their lines. If necessary, students can speak in English first and then Chinese. While reciting their lines, their voices should be loud and clear. It may add interest if students improvise, such as by bowing and joining hands.

Assessment

1. See if students can recite the whole rhyme or part of it.
2. See how many traditional Chinese New Year customs in the rhyme students can explain in their own words.
3. Ask students what other activities they have seen or experienced during Chinese New Year (such as dragon dances or lion dances).

Visit www.cheng-tsui.com for stage prop and costume suggestions by the author. Also, share your own ideas and accomplishments!

The Ants and the Grasshopper

mǎ yǐ hé zhà měng
蚂 蚁 和 蚂 蜢

rén wù
人 物
Characters

mǎ yǐ
蚂 蚁
Ants

zhà měng
蚂 蜢
Grasshopper

jiě shuō yuán
解 说 员
Narrator

Season: Summer and then Autumn **Place:** A field

Act 1

jiě shuō yuán
解 说 员:
Narrator: We are going to tell you the story of "The Ants and the Grasshopper." The story begins on a hot summer day.

(all the Ants run on stage and quickly line up in a half circle)

mǎ yǐ:
蚂 蚁:
Ants:

mǎ yǐ gōng zuò gōng zuò
蚂 蚁 工 作, 工 作,
The Ants are working, working,

gōng zuò
工 作。
working. *(hammering motion with two fists)*

mǎ yǐ lā lā lā
蚂 蚁 拉, 拉, 拉。
The Ants are pulling, pulling, pulling. *(pretending to pull something)*

mǎ yǐ duī duī duī
蚂 蚁 堆, 堆, 堆。
The Ants are stacking, stacking, stacking. *(waving arms above head)*

(Grasshopper enters)

zhà měng:
蚱 蜢:
Grasshopper:

zhà měng lā qín
蚱 蜢 拉 琴。
Grasshopper plays his violin. *(pretends to play a violin and hums a tune)*

zhà měng lā qín
蚱 蜢 拉 琴。
Grasshopper plays his violin. *(pretends to play a violin and hums a tune)*

zhà měng lā qín
蚱蜢 拉 琴。
Grasshopper plays his violin. *(pretends to play a violin and hums a tune)*

nǐ men hǎo
你们 好。
Hello, everybody! *(approaches the Ants)*

mǎ yǐ: nǐ hǎo
蚂蚁： 你 好！
Ants: Hello!

zhà měng: nǐ men máng ma
蚱蜢： 你们 忙 吗？
Grasshopper: Are you guys busy?

mǎ yǐ: shì a wǒ men hěn máng
蚂蚁： 是 啊，我 们 很 忙。
Ants: Yes, we are very busy.

nǐ máng ma
你 忙 吗？
Are you busy?

zhà měng: wǒ bù máng zài jiàn
蚱蜢： 我 不 忙。再 见。
Grasshopper: No, I am not busy. Bye.

mǎ yǐ: zài jiàn
蚂蚁： 再 见。
Ants: Bye.

The Ants and the Grasshopper • 11

mǎ yǐ: 蚂 蚁: **Ants:**	mǎ yǐ gōng zuò gōng zuò 蚂 蚁 工 作，工 作， The Ants are working, working,	

gōng zuò
工 作。
working. *(hammering motion with two fists)*

mǎ yǐ lā lā lā
蚂 蚁 拉，拉，拉。
The Ants are pulling, pulling, pulling. *(pretending to pull something)*

mǎ yǐ duī duī duī
蚂 蚁 堆，堆，堆。
The Ants are stacking, stacking, stacking. *(waving arms above head)*

zhà měng:　　　zhà měng lā qín
蚱 蜢:　　　　蚱 蜢 拉 琴。
Grasshopper:　　Grasshopper plays his violin. *(pretends to play a violin and hums a tune)*

zhà měng lā qín
蚱 蜢 拉 琴。
Grasshopper plays his violin. *(pretends to play a violin and hums a tune)*

zhà měng lā qín
蚱 蜢 拉 琴。
Grasshopper plays his violin. *(pretends to play a violin and hums a tune)*

(Ants approach the Grasshopper)

mǎ yǐ:　　　nǐ hǎo ma
蚂 蚁:　　　你 好 吗？
Ants:　　How are you?

zhà měng:　　wǒ hěn hǎo xiè xie nǐ ne
蚱 蜢:　　　我 很 好，谢 谢。你 呢？
Grasshopper:　　I am very well, thank you. And you?

mǎ yǐ:
蚂 蚁:
Ants:
wǒ men yě hěn hǎo xiè xie
我 们 也 很 好，谢 谢。
We are also fine, thank you.

zài jiàn
再 见。
Bye.

zhà měng:
蚱 蜢:
Grasshopper:
zài jiàn
再 见。
Bye. *(leaves the stage while playing his violin)*

Act 2

jiě shuō yuán
解 说 员:
Narrator: Autumn comes and the weather is getting colder.

mǎ yǐ:
蚂 蚁:
Ants:
mǎ yǐ gōng zuò gōng zuò
蚂 蚁 工 作，工 作，
The Ants are working, working, working.

gōng zuò
工 作。
(hammering motion with two fists)

mǎ yǐ lā lā lā
蚂 蚁 拉，拉，拉。
The Ants are pulling, pulling, pulling. *(pulling something)*

mǎ yǐ duī duī duī
蚂 蚁 堆，堆，堆。
The Ants are stacking, stacking, stacking. *(waving arms above head)*

The Ants and the Grasshopper • 13

zhà měng: 蚱 蜢: Grasshopper:	zhà měng lā qín 蚱 蜢 拉 琴。 Grasshopper plays his violin. *(pretends to play a violin and hums a tune with great enthusiasm)*

zhà měng lā qín
蚱 蜢 拉 琴。
Grasshopper plays his violin. *(pretends to play a violin and hums a tune with less enthusiasm)*

zhà měng lā qín
蚱 蜢 拉 琴。
Grasshopper plays his violin. *(pretends to play a violin and hums a tune with no enthusiasm)*

(Ant 1 approaches the Grasshopper)

mǎ yǐ: 蚂 蚁: Ant 1:	nǐ hǎo zhà měng 你 好, 蚱 蜢。 Hello, Grasshopper.
zhà měng: 蚱 蜢: Grasshopper:	nǐ hǎo 你 好。 Hello. *(sadly)*
mǎ yǐ: 蚂 蚁: Ant 1:	nǐ zěn me le 你 怎 么 了? What's the matter? *(showing concern)*
zhà měng: 蚱 蜢: Grasshopper:	wǒ hěn è 我 很 饿。 I am very hungry. *(points to stomach, shivering)*

mǎ yǐ: **nǐ lěng ma**
蚂 蚁: **你 冷 吗?**
Ant 1: Are you cold? *(showing concern)*

zhà měng: **wǒ hěn lěng**
蚱 蜢: **我 很 冷。**
Grasshopper: I am very cold. *(arms around body, shivering)*

jiě shuō yuán:
解 说 员:
Narrator: Some ants think the grasshopper deserves to be hungry, since he did nothing but play during the summer. Some ants think he deserves another chance. Finally, all of the ants decide to help the grasshopper.

mǎ yǐ: **mǎ yǐ gōng zuò gōng zuò**
蚂 蚁: **蚂 蚁 工 作, 工 作,**
Ants: The Ants are working, working,

gōng zuò
工 作。
working. *(hammering motion with two fists)*

mǎ yǐ lā lā lā
蚂 蚁 拉, 拉, 拉。
The Ants are pulling, pulling, pulling. *(pulling something)*

mǎ yǐ duī duī duī
蚂 蚁 堆, 堆, 堆。
The Ants are stacking, stacking, stacking. *(waving arms above head)*

The Ants and the Grasshopper • 15

mǎ yǐ: zhè shì nǐ de qǐng chī ba
蚂 蚁: 这 是 你 的。请 吃 吧。
Ant 2: This is yours. Please eat it. *(hands Grasshopper a grain of rice)*

zhà měng: xiè xie nǐ
蚱 蜢: 谢 谢 你。
Grasshopper: Thank you.

mǎ yǐ: bú kè qi
蚂 蚁: 不 客 气。
Ant 2: You're welcome.

mǎ yǐ: zhè yě shì nǐ de qǐng chī ba
蚂 蚁: 这 也 是 你 的, 请 吃 吧。
Ant 3: This is also yours. *(hands Grasshopper a grain of rice)* Please eat it.

zhà měng: xiè xie nǐ
蚱 蜢: 谢 谢 你。
Grasshopper: Thank you. *(puts food in his/her mouth)*

mǎ yǐ: bú kè qi
蚂 蚁: 不 客 气。
Ant 3: You're welcome.

mǎ yǐ: zhè dōu shì nǐ de qǐng chī ba
蚂 蚁: 这 都 是 你 的。请 吃 吧。
Ants: All of this is yours. *(ants hand him more rice)* Please eat it.

zhà měng: xiè xie nǐ men yě chī ba
蚱 蜢: 谢 谢。你 们 也 吃 吧。
Grasshopper: Thank you. You have some, too. *(chewing)*

wǒ bǎo le wǒ hé nǐ men
我 饱 了。我 和 你 们
I am full. Let me work

yì qǐ gōng zuò
一 起 工 作。
together with you. *(sincerely)*

mǎ yǐ: hǎo
蚂 蚁: 好。
Ants: All right.

(Grasshopper joins the Ants and works together with them)

mǎ yǐ: mǎ yǐ gōng zuò gōng zuò
蚂 蚁: 蚂 蚁 工 作，工 作，
Ants: The Ants are working, working,

gōng zuò
工 作。
working. *(hammering motion with two fists)*

mǎ yǐ lā lā lā
蚂 蚁 拉，拉，拉。
The Ants are pulling, pulling, pulling. *(pulling something)*

mǎ yǐ duī duī duī
蚂 蚁 堆，堆，堆。
The Ants are stacking, stacking, stacking. *(waving arms above head)*

zhà měng: xiè xie xiè xie
蚱 蜢: 谢 谢。谢 谢。
Grasshopper: Thank you. Thank you.

mǎ yǐ: bú kè qi
蚂 蚁: 不 客 气。
Ants: You're welcome.

jiě shuō yuán:
解 说 员：
Narrator: Soon the grasshopper collects some food for himself and feels happy again. The grasshopper plays his violin again and the ants start to dance.

dà jiā:
大 家：
All:

zhà měng lā qín lā qín lā qín
蚱 蜢 拉 琴，拉 琴，拉 琴。
Grasshopper plays his violin. *(pretends to play a violin)*

mǎ yǐ tiào wǔ tiào wǔ tiào wǔ
蚂 蚁 跳 舞，跳 舞，跳 舞。
The Ants dance. *(two arms above head, spinning)*

zhà měng lā qín lā qín lā qín
蚱 蜢 拉 琴，拉 琴，拉 琴。
Grasshopper plays his violin. *(pretends to play a violin)*

mǎ yǐ tiào wǔ tiào wǔ tiào wǔ
蚂 蚁 跳 舞，跳 舞，跳 舞。
The Ants dance. *(two arms above head, spinning)*

zhà měng lā qín lā qín lā qín
蚱 蜢 拉 琴，拉 琴，拉 琴。
Grasshopper plays his violin. *(pretends to play violin)*

mǎ yǐ tiào wǔ tiào wǔ tiào wǔ
蚂 蚁 跳 舞，跳 舞，跳 舞。
The Ants dance. *(two arms above head, spinning)*

THE END

教学参考

背景介绍

大家知道"蚂蚁和蚱蜢"的寓言教育人们要勤劳,因为不劳是不获的。这个新编的"蚂蚁和蚱蜢"是形体带动说(*TPR)的小品,与原寓言不同之处是蚂蚁们愿意给蚱蜢一个改过的机会。蚂蚁和蚱蜢之间的对话,是初学汉语的学生一定要掌握的问候语。小品可作为一个有趣的课堂活动。当学生熟练掌握后,也可作为全班都参与的气氛热烈的舞台表演。(*TPR)详细解释请看114页。

教学建议

这个小品适用于初学汉语的小学生。小品中蚂蚁的角色有三个动作动词,其中两个动词是单音字,用意是让学生练发音。蚱蜢的角色只有一个动作动词要学会。每个动词在带动说时,要重复三遍。基本的问候和客套话可以事先教会,也可以在情景中教。因为是初学的小学生,解说员的部分可以用英语替换以保证学生说得流畅,亦不会觉得太难。

具体步骤

一、教师用带动说教学生蚂蚁的三个动作动词和蚱蜢的一个动作动词。
二、反复实践这四个动作动词并由教师做问候语的示范。
三、老师当蚂蚁学生当蚱蜢练问候语和礼貌用语并及时交换角色。
四、分小组过小品的脚本并发现各个角色的最佳演员。
五、选定角色,过整个小品的内容。
六、加入唱一个四拍节奏的旋律来呼应蚱蜢拉琴的表演。

舞台表演

蚂蚁和蚱蜢形体带动说小品中的建议

一、蚂蚁工作:拳头紧握,左拳在下,右拳在上,捶打三下。
二、蚂蚁拉:拳头紧握,在胸前有节奏地从左上方向右下方拉三下。
三、蚂蚁堆:举起双手,从左到右有节奏地摆动三下。
四、蚱蜢拉琴:做拉小提琴的动作后,唱一个四拍的旋律。例如:{5i ii 76 5}

五、蚂蚁跳舞:举起双手,原地转动一圈,像在跳舞。
六、结尾:演员一对一对地走到台前,鞠躬后向观众说再见。

评估

一、学生能正确使用情节中的行为动词。
二、学生能在其他场合正确使用问候语和礼貌用语。

请上网 www.cheng-tsui.com 查看作者有关道具制作和选用服装的建议。也请您与大家分享您的好主意和成果。

Teaching Reference

Background Information

The fable "The Ants and the Grasshopper" tells people that hard work brings rewards. In it, the industrious ants store up food for the winter while the laid-back grasshopper goes hungry. This version differs from the original story in that the ants help the grasshopper by sharing their food. The grasshopper, in turn, gives something back to the ants.

This dramatic version of the fable is retold using a Total Physical Response (TPR) form of storytelling. Action verbs are acted out by a group of ants and the grasshopper, while the rest of the students (the army of ants) follow suit by repeating the actions. It can be a fun in-class activity or stage performance involving the entire class. (For further explanation about TPR, see page 115.

Teaching Suggestions

This skit is designed for younger students at the elementary level. There are three action verbs for the ants and one action verb for the grasshopper. Each action verb will be repeated three times. Basic greetings can be introduced separately or through the roles of the ants and the grasshopper in the skit. The narrator's English role can be played by one of the ants.

Preparatory Steps

1. Tell the story by acting out all the roles and demonstrating the movements for the action verbs "work," "pull," and "stack." When students understand the story, they should respond by mimicking the teacher's actions.
2. Practice as many times as needed until students gradually take over the lines and action verbs.
3. The teacher plays the ants while the students play the grasshopper, and vice versa.
4. Students take turns playing the grasshopper and the narrator so that nobody feels left out.
5. Divide the class into two parts to practice the dialogues and act out "work," "pull," and "stack"
6. Hum a tune together with the grasshopper every time the narrator says "grasshopper plays the violin" in Chinese.

Stage Performance: Suggestions for Total Physical Response Actions

1. The Ants are working: right fist on top of left fist, mimicking the action of a hammer hitting a nail.
2. The Ants are pulling: two fists pulling diagonally in front of one's chest three times, as if engaged in a tug-of-war.
3. The Ants are stacking: two arms above head and wave from right to left three times, to mimic the action of lifting something up and placing it on top of a pile.
4. The Grasshopper plays the violin: pretending to play a violin while humming a tune. (For example, in the key of C Major, the tune might go "GC CC BA G")

5. The Ants dance: pirouetting with both arms above the head.
6. At the end, performers appear in pairs and say "thank you" and "goodbye" to the audience.

Assessment

1. Students will be able to use the action verbs "work," "pull," and "stack" in appropriate situations.
2. Students will be able to use greetings and polite language when speaking with others.

Visit www.cheng-tsui.com for stage prop and costume suggestions by the author. Also, share your own ideas and accomplishments!

THE LITTLE TADPOLES LOOK FOR THEIR MOTHER

xiǎo kē dǒu zhǎo mā ma
小 蝌 蚪 找 妈 妈

rén wù
人 物
Characters

jiě shuō yuán 解 说 员 **Narrator**	xiǎo huā niú 小 花 牛 **Little (Black and White) Calf**
sān duǒ xiǎo làng huā 三 朵 小 浪 花 **Three Little Waves**	wǔ zhī xiǎo kē dǒu 五 只 小 蝌 蚪 **Five Little Tadpoles**
xiǎo shān yáng 小 山 羊 **Little Goat**	dà qīng wā 大 青 蛙 **Big Frog**
xiǎo tù zi 小 兔 子 **Little Rabbit**	xiǎo wū guī 小 乌 龟 **Little Turtle**
xiǎo yā zi 小 鸭 子 **Little Duck**	

Season: Spring　　　**Place:** At the edge of a pond

Act 1

jiě shuō yuán:
解说员:
Narrator:

wǒ men biǎo yǎn de jié mù shì
我们表演的节目是
We are going to perform

xiǎo kē dǒu zhǎo mā ma
"小蝌蚪找妈妈"。
"The Little Tadpoles Look for Their Mother."

xiǎo làng huā yī:
小浪花一:
Little Wave 1:

wǒ shì xiǎo làng huā
我是小浪花。
I am a Little Wave. Hello,

nǐ men hǎo
你们好!
everyone!

xiǎo làng huā èr:
小浪花二:
Little Wave 2:

wǒ yě shì xiǎo làng huā
我也是小浪花。
I am a Little Wave, too.

nǐ men hǎo
你们好!
Hello, everyone!

xiǎo làng huā sān:
小浪花三:
Little Wave 3:

nǐ men hǎo
你们好!
Hello, everyone!

wǒ shì xiǎo làng huā
我是小浪花。
I am a Little Wave.

xiǎo shān yáng: wǒ shì xiǎo shān yáng
小山羊： 我是小山羊。
Little Goat: I am a Little Goat.

nǐ men hǎo
你们好！
Hello, everyone!

xiǎo tù zi: wǒ shì xiǎo tù zi nǐ men hǎo
小兔子： 我是小兔子。你们好！
Little Rabbit: I am a Little Rabbit. Hello, everyone!

xiǎo yā zi: wǒ shì xiǎo yā zi nǐ men hǎo
小鸭子： 我是小鸭子。你们好！
Little Duck: I am a Little Duck. Hello, everyone!

xiǎo huā niú: wǒ shì xiǎo huā niú nǐ men hǎo
小花牛： 我是小花牛。你们好！
Little Calf: I am a Little Calf. Hello, everyone!

xiǎo wū guī: wǒ shì xiǎo wū guī nǐ men hǎo
小乌龟： 我是小乌龟。你们好！
Little Turtle: I am a Little Turtle. Hello, everyone!

kē dǒu yī: nǐ men hǎo wǒ shì xiǎo kē dǒu
蝌蚪一： 你们好！我是小蝌蚪。
Little Tadpole 1: Hello, everyone! I am a Little Tadpole.

kē dǒu èr: nǐ men hǎo
蝌蚪二： 你们好！
Little Tadpole 2: Hello, everyone!

wǒ yě shì xiǎo kē dǒu
我也是小蝌蚪。
I am a Little Tadpole, too.

The Little Tadpoles Look for Their Mother • 25

蝌蚪三: (kē dǒu sān)
我是小蝌蚪。你们好！ (wǒ shì xiǎo kē dǒu nǐ men hǎo)
Little Tadpole 3: I am a Little Tadpole. Hello, everyone!

蝌蚪四: (kē dǒu sì)
我也是小蝌蚪。 (wǒ yě shì xiǎo kē dǒu)
Little Tadpole 4: I am a Little Tadpole, too.

你们好！ (nǐ men hǎo)
Hello, everyone!

蝌蚪五: (kē dǒu wǔ)
你们好！我是小蝌蚪。 (nǐ men hǎo wǒ shì xiǎo kē dǒu)
Little Tadpole 5: Hello, everyone! I am a Little Tadpole.

我要找妈妈。 (wǒ yào zhǎo mā ma)
I want to find my mother.

蝌蚪们: (kē dǒu men)
我们都要找妈妈。 (wǒ men dōu yào zhǎo mā ma)
Little Tadpoles: We all want to find our mother.

Act 2

小浪花: (xiǎo làng huā)
小蝌蚪游啊游，游啊游。 (xiǎo kē dǒu yóu a yóu yóu a yóu)
Little Waves: The Little Tadpoles are swimming and swimming.

蝌蚪一: (kē dǒu yī)
小山羊，你是我妈妈吗？ (xiǎo shān yáng nǐ shì wǒ mā ma ma)
Little Tadpole 1: Little Goat, are you my mom?

小山羊: (xiǎo shān yáng)
对不起,我不是你妈妈。
duì bù qǐ wǒ bú shì nǐ mā ma
Little Goat: Sorry, I am not your mom.

你的妈妈有大眼睛。
nǐ de mā mā yǒu dà yǎn jing
Your mom has big eyes.

蝌蚪一: (kē dǒu yī)
噢,我的妈妈有大
òu wǒ de mā ma yǒu dà
Little Tadpole 1: Oh, my mom has big

眼睛。谢谢。再见。
yǎn jing xiè xie zài jiàn
eyes. Thank you. Goodbye.

小山羊: (xiǎo shān yang)
再见。
zài jiàn
Little Goat: Goodbye.

小浪花: (xiǎo làng huā)
小蝌蚪游啊游,游啊游。
xiǎo kē dǒu yóu a yóu yóu a yóu
Little Waves: The Little Tadpoles are swimming and swimming.

蝌蚪二: (kē dǒu èr)
小兔子,你是我妈妈吗?
xiǎo tù zi nǐ shì wǒ mā ma ma
Little Tadpoles 2: Little Rabbit, are you my mom?

xiǎo tù zi:
小 兔子:
Little Rabbit:

duì bù qǐ wǒ bú shì nǐ mā ma
对不起,我不是你妈妈。
Sorry, I am not your mom.

nǐ de mā ma yǒu dà zuǐ ba
你的妈妈有大嘴巴。
Your mom has a large mouth.

kē dǒu èr:
蝌蚪二:
Little Tadpole 2:

òu wǒ de mā ma yǒu dà zuǐ ba
噢,我的妈妈有大嘴巴。
Oh, my mom has a large mouth.

xiè xie zài jiàn
谢谢,再见。
Thanks, goodbye.

xiǎo tù zi:
小 兔子:
Little Rabbit:

zài jiàn
再见。
Goodbye.

xiǎo làng huā:
小 浪花:
Little Waves:

xiǎo kē dǒu yóu a yóu yóu a yóu
小蝌蚪游啊游,游啊游。
The Little Tadpoles are swimming and swimming.

kē dǒu sān:
蝌蚪三:
Little Tadpole 3:

xiǎo yā zi
小鸭子,
Little Duck,

nǐ shì wǒ mā ma ma
你是我妈妈吗?
are you my mom?

xiǎo yā zi: 小鸭子:
Little Duck:

bú shì bú shì
不是，不是。
No, I'm not.

wǒ bú shì nǐ de mā ma
我不是你的妈妈。
I am not your mom.

nǐ de mā ma yǒu sì tiáo tuǐ
你的妈妈有四条腿。
Your mom has four legs.

kē dǒu sān: 蝌蚪三:
Little Tadpole 3:

òu wǒ de mā ma yǒu sì tiáo tuǐ
噢，我的妈妈有四条腿。
Oh, my mom has four legs.

xiè xie zài jiàn
谢谢。再见。
Thanks. Bye.

xiǎo yā zi: 小鸭子:
Little Duck:

zài jiàn
再见。
Bye.

xiǎo làng huā: 小浪花:
Little Waves:

xiǎo kē dǒu yóu a yóu yóu a yóu
小蝌蚪游啊游，游啊游。
The Little Tadpoles are swimming and swimming.

kē dǒu sì: 蝌蚪四:
Little Tadpole 4:

xiǎo huā niú
小花牛，
Little Calf,

nǐ shì wǒ māma ma
你是我妈妈吗？
are you my mom?

xiǎo huā niú:
小花牛：
Little Calf:

duì bù qǐ wǒ bú shì nǐ māma
对不起，我不是你妈妈。
I am sorry, I am not your mother.

nǐ de māma chuān lǜ yī fu
你的妈妈穿绿衣服。
Your mom wears green clothes.

kē dǒu sì:
蝌蚪四：
Little Tadpole 4:

òu wǒ de māma chuān lǜ yī fu
噢，我的妈妈穿绿衣服。
Oh, my mom wears green clothes.

xiè xie zài jiàn
谢谢。再见。
Thanks. Bye.

xiǎo huā niú:
小花牛：
Little Calf:

zài jiàn
再见。
Goodbye.

xiǎo làng huā:
小浪花：
Little Waves:

xiǎo kē dǒu yóu a yóu
小蝌蚪游啊游,
The Little Tadpoles are swimming

yóu a yóu
游啊游。
and swimming.

kē dǒu wǔ: 蝌蚪五: Little Tadpole 5:
xiǎo wū guī nǐ shì wǒ mā ma ma
小乌龟,你是我妈妈吗?
Little Turtle, are you my mom?

xiǎo wū guī: 小乌龟: Little Turtle:
bú shì bú shì
不是,不是,
No, no,

wǒ bú shì nǐ mā ma
我不是你妈妈。
I am not your mom.

nǐ de mā ma ài chàng gē
你的妈妈爱唱歌。
Your mom likes to sing.

kē dǒu wǔ: 蝌蚪五: Little Tadpole 5:
òu wǒ de mā ma ài chàng gē
噢,我的妈妈爱唱歌。
Oh, my mom likes to sing.

xiè xie zài jiàn
谢谢。再见。
Thank you. Goodbye.

xiǎo wū guī: 小乌龟: Little Turtle:
zài jiàn
再见。
Goodbye.

The Little Tadpoles Look for Their Mother

Act 3

dà qīng wā: guā guā guā, guā guā guā
大 青 蛙: 呱 呱 呱, 呱 呱 呱。
Big Frog: Ribbit, ribbit, ribbit.

wǒ shì kē dǒu de mā ma
我 是 蝌 蚪 的 妈 妈。
I am the tadpoles' mother.

guā guā guā, guā guā guā
呱 呱 呱, 呱 呱 呱。
Ribbit, ribbit, ribbit.

kē dǒu yī: dà yǎn jing
蝌 蚪 一: 大 眼 睛。
Little Tadpole 1:   Big eyes. *(looking at Big Frog)*

xiǎo kē dǒu: dà yǎn jing
小 蝌 蚪: 大 眼 睛。
Little Tadpoles: Big eyes.

kē dǒu èr: dà zuǐ ba
蝌 蚪 二: 大 嘴 巴。
Little Tadpole 2:   Large mouth.

xiǎo kē dǒu: dà zuǐ ba
小 蝌 蚪: 大 嘴 巴。
Little Tadpoles: Large mouth.

kē dǒu sān: sì tiáo tuǐ
蝌 蚪 三: 四 条 腿。
Little Tadpole 3:   Four legs. *(looking at Big Frog)*

小蝌蚪 Little Tadpoles: sì tiáo tuǐ 四条腿。 Four legs.

蝌蚪四 Little Tadpole 4: lǜ yī fu 绿衣服。 Green clothes.

小蝌蚪 Little Tadpoles: lǜ yī fu 绿衣服。 Green clothes.

蝌蚪五 Little Tadpole 5: nín hǎo nín shì wǒ men de mā ma ma 您好!您是我们的妈妈吗? Hello! Are you our mother?

大青蛙 Big Frog: shì shì hái zi men 是,是。孩子们, Yes, yes. Children,

wǒ shì nǐ men de mā ma 我是你们的妈妈。 I am your mother. *(puts arms around Tadpoles)*

小蝌蚪 Little Tadpoles: hǎo a wǒ men zhǎo dào mā ma le 好啊!我们找到妈妈了。 Good! We have found our mother. *(clap hands)*

wǒ men zhǎo dào mā ma le 我们找到妈妈了! We have found our mother!

The Little Tadpoles Look for Their Mother

Act 4

All: *(clap hands three times and recite closing rhyme together)*

xiǎo kē dǒu yóu a yóu
小 蝌 蚪 游 啊 游，
Little tadpoles swim and swim, *(pretending to swim)*

yóu dào dōng yóu dào xī
游 到 东 游 到 西。
swim to the east and swim to the west. *(turning to the right and then to the left)*

zhǎo mā ma zhēn zhāo jí
找 妈 妈 真 着 急，
They are anxious to find their mother,

mā ma nǐ zài nǎ lǐ
妈 妈，你 在 哪 里？
Mom, where are you? *(two hands in front of mouth)*

xiǎo kē dǒu yóu a yóu
小 蝌 蚪 游 啊 游，
Little tadpoles swim and swim,

yóu dào dōng yóu dào xī
游 到 东 游 到 西。
swim to the east and swim to the west.

zhǎo mā ma zhēn zháo jí
找 妈 妈 真 着 急。
They are anxious to find their mother.

mā ma nǐ zài zhè lǐ
妈 妈，你 在 这 里！
Mom, you are here! *(pointing to Big Frog)*

THE END

教学参考

背景介绍

"小蝌蚪找妈妈"是中国著名童话故事之一。

这里的小品"小蝌蚪找妈妈"是根据这个童话故事改编的。改编的目的是希望这个小品的脚本适合舞台表演。学生可以通过舞台上的情景学会问答一个最基本的"吗"字句型。小品中"你是我妈妈吗?"这个问题反反复复地出现,为学生提供一个汉语是怎么对话的感性认知。

教学建议

这个小品适用于初学汉语的学生。如果学生已经知道五官和四肢的词汇,对基本的一般疑问句的语法现象也有所了解的话,教学从复习阅读入手。如果班上学生较多,让两个学生挑选一个角色来表演也会有很好的效果。学生掌握台词的时间不等,让掌握快些的学生做示范。挑选三个较负责任的学生当"小浪花",因为这个角色实际上是整个小品表演的指挥。

具体步骤

一、复习小品中的词汇或者用"咪咪说"(105页)来教五官和四肢的词汇。
二、选择各自的角色并开始大声朗读台词。
三、过脚本的台词并及时纠正学生的语音和语调。
四、回答学生对小品中的问题并要求学生逐步能背诵各自的台词。
五、学生按照脚本台词的顺序走上舞台并能使用麦克风。

舞台表演

演员在舞台上表演结束时的位置(参考)

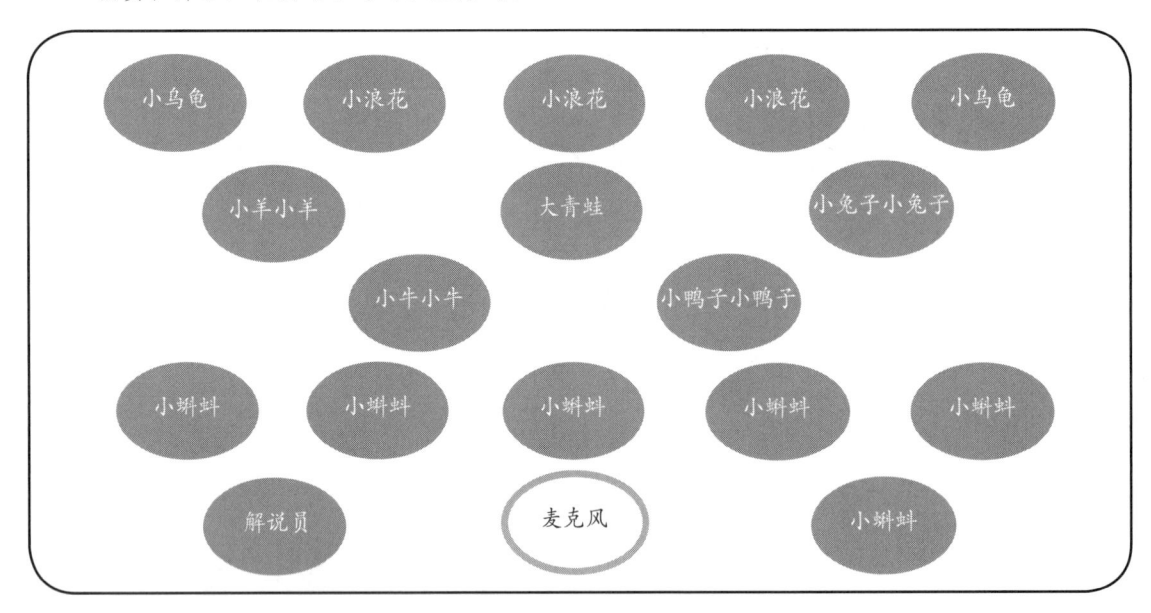

小乌龟	小浪花	小浪花	小浪花	小乌龟
小羊小羊		大青蛙		小兔子小兔子
	小牛小牛		小鸭子小鸭子	
小蝌蚪	小蝌蚪	小蝌蚪	小蝌蚪	小蝌蚪
解说员		麦克风		小蝌蚪

评估小结

一、学生知道怎么使用"你是...吗?"的问句。
二、讨论这个童话故事想告诉我们什么。

请上网www.cheng-tsui.com查看作者有关道具制作和选用服装的建议。也请您与大家分享您的好主意和成果。

Teaching Reference

Background Information

"The Little Tadpoles Look for Their Mother" is one of the most popular Chinese fairy tales. In this skit based on the fairy tale, performers learn important basic sentence structures. Questions ending with ma, and answers to these questions, are repeated throughout the skit, providing an opportunity for performers to conduct a question and answer dialogue in Chinese. The three "Little Waves" act as a chorus.

Teaching Suggestions

The stage version of this fairy tale is suitable for a class of ten to twenty beginning-level students. Let students work in pairs to practice the entire skit several times. While learning times vary from student to student, performers get the chance to practice the skit over and over again. Select three students who are eager to play the role of the three Little Waves. This role is actually the chorus of the skit.

Preparatory Steps

1. Review the vocabulary in the skit. (Use the activity "Mimi Says" on page 105 for this).
2. Pair students together. Assign roles and let each pair read the entire skit out loud by alternating lines.
3. Assist each pair of students with pronunciation and intonation.
4. When the class is back together in a large group, answer students' questions and go over the whole skit.
5. Make sure students are comfortable speaking into a microphone.

Stage Performance

Listed below is a chart for arranging stage performers.

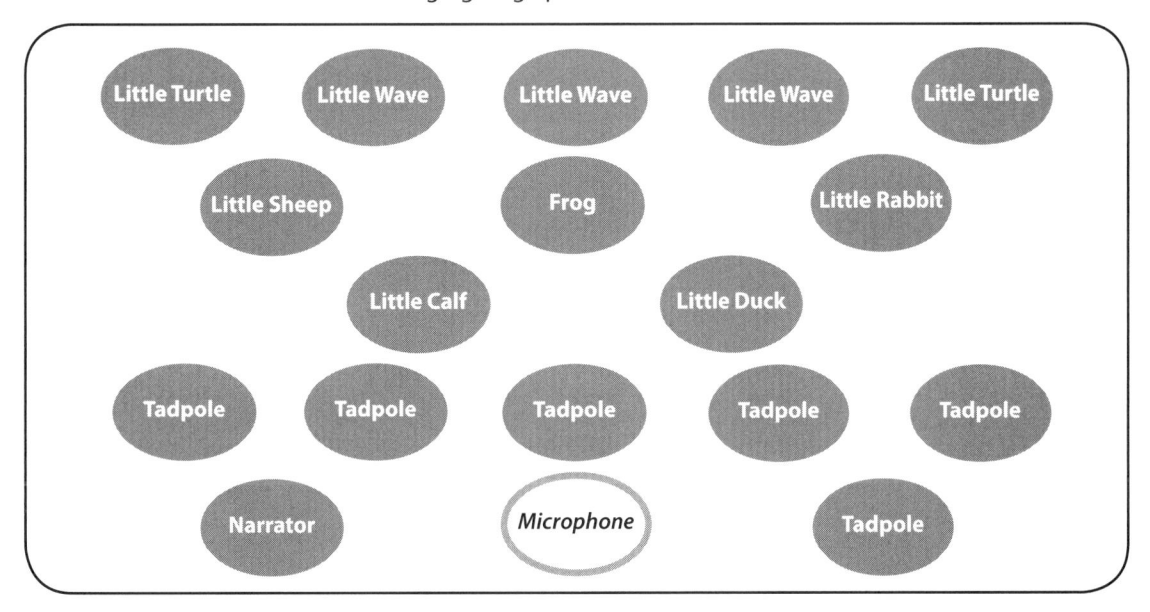

```
 Little Turtle   Little Wave    Little Wave    Little Wave    Little Turtle

    Little Sheep         Frog              Little Rabbit

            Little Calf        Little Duck

  Tadpole   Tadpole   Tadpole   Tadpole   Tadpole

        Narrator    Microphone        Tadpole
```

Assessment

1. See if students can ask and answer questions in other situations.
2. Discuss the meaning of the fairy tale.

Visit www.cheng-tsui.com for stage prop and costume suggestions by the author.
Also, share your own ideas and accomplishments!

THE TURTLE AND THE HARE

guī tù sài pǎo
龟 兔 赛 跑

rén wù
人 物
Characters

jiě shuō yuán 解 说 员 **Narrator**	wū guī dì di 乌 龟 弟 弟 **Turtle's Little Brother**
tù zi wū guī 兔 子 乌 龟 **Hare** **Turtle**	wū guī mèi mei 乌 龟 妹 妹 **Turtle's Little Sister**
tù zi gē ge 兔 子 哥 哥 **Hare's Big Brother**	wū guī mā ma 乌 龟 妈 妈 **Turtle's Mother**
tù zi jiě jie 兔 子 姐 姐 **Hare's Big Sister**	tù zi mā ma 兔 子 妈 妈 **Hare's Mother**

Season: Autumn **Place:** A forest

Act 1 — Before the Race

jiě shuō yuán: lán lán de tiān
解 说 员： 蓝 蓝 的 天，
Narrator: Blue sky and

(stretches arms toward the sky and walks around the stage to catch audience's eyes)

bái bái de yún, sēn lín shēn chù
白 白 的 云，森 林 深 处
white clouds appear deep in the forest,

xiǎo niǎo fēi lái fēi qù zài bào
小 鸟 飞 来 飞 去 在 报
and birds fly back and forth to report

gào yí gè xiāo xi nǐ men zhī
告 一 个 消 息。你 们 知
a piece of news. Do you know

dào shì shén me xiāo xi ma
道 是 什 么 消 息 吗？
what news that is? *(speaking to audience)*

(waits for the audience to give an answer by pushing one ear forward, then says)

wū guī hé tù zi yào sài pǎo
乌 龟 和 兔 子 要 赛 跑！
Turtle and Hare are going to have a race!

dà jiā kuài lái yā
大 家 快 来 呀！
Come on, everybody!

wū guī dì di:
乌龟弟弟:
Turtle's Little Brother:

wǒ shì wū guī de dì di
我 是 乌 龟 的 弟 弟。
I am Turtle's little brother. *(seriously)*

gē ge hé tù zi yào sài
哥 哥 和 兔 子 要 赛
Big Brother and Hare are going to

pǎo nǐ men bié xiào shéi shū
跑。你 们 别 笑。谁 输
race. Please do not laugh. Who will lose and

shéi yíng hái bù zhī dào
谁 赢？还 不 知 道。
who will win? We still do not know.

tù zi gē ge:
兔子哥哥:
Hare's Big Brother:

wǒ shì tù zi de gē ge
我 是 兔 子 的 哥 哥。
I am Hare's big brother. *(humorously)*

dì di hé wū guī yào sài
弟 弟 和 乌 龟 要 赛
Little Brother and Turtle are going to race.

pǎo nǐ men bié xiào shéi shū
跑。你 们 别 笑。谁 输
Please do not laugh. Who will lose and

shéi yíng yǐ jīng zhī dào
谁 赢？已 经 知 道。
who will win? We already know.

wū guī mèi mei:
乌龟妹妹:
Turtle's Little Sister:

wǒ shì wū guī de mèi mei
我 是 乌 龟 的 妹 妹。
I am Turtle's little sister. *(seriously)*

gē ge hé tù zi yào sài
哥哥和兔子要赛
Big Brother and Hare are going to

pǎo nǐ men bié xiào shéi shū
跑。你们别笑。谁输
race. Please do not laugh. Who will lose and

shéi yíng hái bù zhī dào
谁赢？还不知道。
who will win? We still do not know.

tù zi jiě jie:
兔子姐姐:
Hare's Big Sister:

wǒ shì tù zi de jiě jie
我是兔子的姐姐。
I am Hare's big sister. *(humorously)*

dì di hé wū guī yào sài
弟弟和乌龟要赛
Little Brother and Turtle are going to

pǎo nǐ men bié xiào shéi shū
跑。你们别笑。谁输
race. Please do not laugh. Who will lose and

shéi yíng yǐ jīng zhī dào
谁赢？已经知道。
who will win? We already know.

(Little Turtle's and Little Rabbit's siblings recite the following rhyme)

dà jiā yī:
大家一:
Group 1 (Little Turtle's Siblings):

xiǎo wū guī bù tíng bù
小乌龟不停步，
Little Turtle is plodding along,

yì shēn hàn máng gǎn lù
一身汗忙赶路。
sweating all over as he goes.

dà jiā èr:
大家二:
Group 2 (Little Rabbit's Siblings):

xiǎo tù zi pǎo de kuài
小 兔 子 跑 得 快，
Little Rabbit runs fast,

ná dì yī bù qí guài
拿 第 一 不 奇 怪。
for him to win would be no surprise.

dà jiā yī:
大家一:
Group 1 (Little Turtle's Siblings):

xiǎo wū guī bù tíng bù
小 乌 龟 不 停 步，
Little Turtle is plodding along,

yì shēn hàn máng gǎn lù
一 身 汗 忙 赶 路。
sweating all over as he goes.

xiǎo tù zi pǎo de kuài
小 兔 子 跑 得 快，
Little Rabbit runs fast,

ná dì yī bù qí guài
拿 第 一 不 奇 怪。
for him to win would be no surprise.

(Little Turtle and Little Hare's siblings exit. Little Turtle's Mother and Little Hare's Mother continue speaking)

wū guī mā ma:
乌龟妈妈:
Turtle's Mother:

wǒ shì wū guī de mā ma
我 是 乌 龟 的 妈 妈。
I am Turtle's mother. *(proudly)*

xiǎo wū guī hé tù zi yào
小 乌 龟 和 兔 子 要
Little Turtle and Hare are going to

赛跑。你们别笑。谁
sài pǎo nǐ men bié xiào shéi
race. Please do not laugh. Who will lose and

输 谁 赢？还 不 知 道。
shū shéi yíng hái bù zhī dào
who will win? We still do not know.

tù zi mā ma: / 兔子妈妈： / Hare's Mother:

我 是 兔 子 的 妈 妈。
wǒ shì tù zi de mā ma
I am Hare's mother. *(proudly)*

小 兔 子 和 乌 龟 要
xiǎo tù zi hé wū guī yào
Little Hare and Turtle are going to

赛 跑。你 们 别 笑。谁
sài pǎo nǐ men bié xiào shéi
race. Please do not laugh. Who will lose and

输 谁 赢？已 经 知 道。
shū shéi yíng yǐ jīng zhī dào
who will win? We already know

(Little Turtle and Little Hare come to the front of the stage, and their family members move back)

wū guī: / 乌龟： / Turtle:

今 天 我 和 兔 子 要
jīn tiān wǒ hé tù zi yào
Today I am going to race Hare. *(proudly and seriously)*

赛 跑。你 们 别 笑。谁
sài pǎo nǐ men bié xiào shéi
Please do not laugh. Who will lose and

输 谁 赢？还 不 知 道。
shū shéi yíng hái bù zhī dào
who will win? We still do not know. *(walks slowly, head down)*

兔子: 今天我和乌龟要赛跑。你们别笑。谁输谁赢？已经知道。

Hare: I am going to race Turtle today. *(proudly and relaxed)* Please do not laugh. Who will lose and who will win? We already know. *(runs in place and then quickly runs away)*

(Group 1, Little Turtle and his/her family, recite the following rhyme as they wait for the race to begin)

大家一: 小乌龟不停步，一身汗忙赶路。

Group 1: Little Turtle keeps plodding along, sweating all over as he goes.

(Group 2, Little Rabbit and his/her family, recite the following rhyme as they wait for the race to begin)

大家二: 小兔子跑得快，拿第一不奇怪。

Group 2: Little Rabbit runs fast, for him to win would be no surprise.

大家一: 小乌龟不停步，

Group 1: Little Turtle keeps plodding along,

<pre>
              yì   shēn hàn   máng gǎn   lù
              一   身   汗   忙   赶   路。
              sweating all over as he goes.
</pre>

dà jiā èr:	xiǎo tù zi pǎo de kuài
大家二:	小 兔 子 跑 得 快,
Group 2:	Little Rabbit runs fast,

<pre>
              ná   dì   yī   bù   qí   guài
              拿   第   一   不   奇   怪。
              for him to win would be no surprise.
</pre>

Act 2 The Race

jiě shuō yuán:	guī tù sài pǎo xiàn zài kāi shǐ
解 说 员:	龟 兔 赛 跑 现 在 开 始!
Narrator:	The race between Turtle and Hare now begins! *(blows a whistle)*

(performers take their places on the stage in preparation for the race)

dà jiā:	tù zi pǎo sōu sōu sōu
大 家:	兔 子 跑, 嗖 嗖 嗖。
All:	Hare runs, whizzing right by.

<pre>
              wū   guī   zǒu   màn   yōu   yōu
              乌   龟   走,   慢   悠   悠。
              Turtle walks, ever so slowly.

              tù   zi   pǎo   sōu   sōu   sōu
              兔   子   跑,   嗖   嗖   嗖。
              Hare runs, whizzing right by.
</pre>

wū guī zǒu màn yōu yōu
乌龟走，慢悠悠。
Turtle walks, ever so slowly.

tù zi gē ge:
兔子哥哥：
Hare's Big Brother:

tù zi kàn jiàn wū guī
兔子看见乌龟
Hare sees Turtle

luò zài hòu biān
落在后边。
fall behind.

(Hare stretches neck and looks back)

tù zi:
兔子：
Hare:

wǒ kuài wǒ bàng wǒ kě le
我快！我棒！我渴了。
I am fast! I am great! I am thirsty.

tù zi jiě jie:
兔子姐姐：
Hare's Big Sister:

tù zi hē shuǐ hū hū hā
兔子喝水，呼呼哈。
Hare drinks water. *(pretends to gulp down a glass of water)*

tù zi mā ma:
兔子妈妈：
Hare's Mother:

tù zi kàn jiàn wū guī gǎn
兔子看见乌龟赶
Hare sees Turtle catching

shàng lái
上来。
up.

tù zi:
兔子：
Hare:

wǒ děi zǒu le
我得走了。
I must go.

dà jiā:
大家：
All:

tù zi pǎo sōu sōu sōu
兔子跑，嗖嗖嗖。
Hare runs, whizzing right by.

The Turtle and the Hare

wū guī zǒu màn yōu yōu
乌龟走，慢悠悠。
Turtle walks, ever so slowly.

tù zi pǎo sōu sōu sōu
兔子跑，嗖嗖嗖。
Hare runs, whizzing right by.

wū guī zǒu màn yōu yōu
乌龟走，慢悠悠。
Turtle walks, ever so slowly.

wū guī dì di:
乌龟弟弟：
Turtle's Little Brother:

tù zi yǐ wéi wū guī
兔子以为乌龟
Hare sees Turtle

luò zài hòu biān
落在后边。
fall behind.

tù zi:
兔子：
Hare:

wǒ kuài wǒ bàng wǒ è le
我快！我棒！我饿了！
I am fast! I am great! I am hungry!

wū guī mèi mei:
乌龟妹妹：
Turtle's Little Sister:

tù zi chī luó bo hǎo chī
兔子吃萝卜，好吃！
Hare eats a turnip, yummy!

wū guī mā ma:
乌龟妈妈：
Turtle's Mother:

tù zi kàn jiàn wū guī gǎn
兔子看见乌龟赶
Hare sees Turtle catching

shàng lái
上来。
up.

tù zi: wǒ děi zǒu le
兔子: 我得走了。
Hare: I must go.

dà jiā: tù zi pǎo sōu sōu sōu
大家: 兔子跑，嗖嗖嗖。
All: Hare runs, whizzing right by.

wū guī zǒu màn yōu yōu
乌龟走，慢悠悠。
Turtle walks, ever so slowly.

tù zi pǎo sōu sōu sōu
兔子跑，嗖嗖嗖。
Hare runs, whizzing right by.

wū guī zǒu màn yōu yōu
乌龟走，慢悠悠。
Turtle walks, ever so slowly.

jiě shuō yuán: tù zi kàn jiàn wū guī luò zài
解说员: 兔子看见乌龟落在
Narrator: Hare sees Turtle fall

hòu biān
后边。
behind.

tù zi: wǒ kuài wǒ bàng wǒ kùn le
兔子: 我快！我棒！我困了。
Hare: I am fast! I am great! I am sleepy. *(yawns)*

dà jiā:
大家:
All:

tù zi shuì jiào hū hū hū
兔子睡觉，呼呼呼。
Hare is sleeping. *(makes a snoring sound)*

tù zi shuì jiào hū hū hū
兔子睡觉，呼呼呼。
Hare is sleeping. *(makes a snoring sound)*

wū guī zǒu màn yōu yōu
乌龟走，慢悠悠。
Turtle walks, ever so slowly.

wū guī zǒu màn yōu yōu
乌龟走，慢悠悠。
Turtle walks, ever so slowly. *(speaking quickly)*

wū guī chāo guò le tù zi
乌龟超过了兔子。
Turtle has passed Hare. *(quietly)*

tù zi shuì jiào hū hū hū
兔子睡觉，呼呼呼。
Hare is sleeping. *(makes a snoring sound)*

wū guī zǒu màn yōu yōu
乌龟走，慢悠悠。
Turtle walks, ever so slowly. *(speaking more quickly)*

jiě shuō yuán:
解说员:
Narrator:

wū guī jiù yào dào zhōng diǎn xiàn le
乌龟就要到终点线了。
Turtle is about to reach the finish line.

tù zi kàn jiàn wū guī hái méi
兔子看见乌龟还没
Hare thinks that Turtle has not yet

<pre>
                        gǎn shàng lái
                        赶   上   来。
                        caught up.

tù zi: wū guī nǐ zài nǎ lǐ ne
兔 子：   乌   龟，你 在   哪 里 呢？
Hare: Turtle, where are you? (looking back, with a mocking voice)

wū guī: wǒ zài zhè lǐ
乌   龟：   我   在   这   里。
Turtle: I am right here. (one step away from the finish line)

dà jiā: tù zi pǎo sōu sōu sōu
大 家：   兔 子 跑， 嗖   嗖   嗖。
All: Hare runs, whizzing right by. (Hare stands right behind Turtle)

wū guī: wǒ yíng le
乌   龟：   我   赢   了！
Turtle: I won! (proudly, with head held high)

tù zi: wǒ shū le zhēn zāo gāo
兔 子：   我   输   了！真   糟   糕！
Hare: I lost. Oh, no!

dà jiā: xiǎo tù zi pǎo de kuài
大 家：   小   兔 子 跑   得 快，
All: Little Hare runs fast,

               ná dì èr bù qí guài
               拿 第 二 不 奇 怪。
               that he came in second is no surprise.
</pre>

THE END

教学参考

背景介绍：

　　这个小品是根据"龟兔赛跑"的寓言故事改编的。小品的特点是以带动说，即(TPR)的方法，来讲故事。小乌龟们和小兔子们还分别站出来表明他们的观点，寓言的用意自在其中。学生对所熟悉的故事中的词汇感兴趣也学得较快。小品可以作为有趣的课堂活动或是全班都可以上场表演的节目。小品有龟兔赛跑前和龟兔赛跑两个部分。

教学建议

　　小品的第一部分是每一个人的亮相。一个一个地走上台向观众介绍自己并说明对龟兔赛跑的观点。不管班上是六个学生还是十几个学生，可以用一对儿或三人一组的方法来调整。每个角色有各自的独白，独白的句子大体都是一样的。教一遍学生即可举一反三。

　　第二部分是集体带动说表演的部分。所有台上的学生要带动说(TPR)小品中的两个动作动词，"兔子跑，龟兔走"，从开始到结束。学生需要练习一起说得有节奏和做协调的动作。兔子的角色任务最重，要挑选善于表演和外向的学生来担任。一般情况下，学演这个小品需要三个课时和三个家庭作业的时间来完成。带动说的动作要和学生们约定好，固定的动作表示一个固定的动词，学生们可以通过带动说(TPR)，学说话和记忆整个小品的内容。

具体步骤

一、利用带动说，学动作动词和四句歌谣。
二、学生挑选角色并大声朗读各自的独白部分。
三、教师示范表演小品并及时纠正学生的语音语调。
四、过小品的脚本并鼓励学生逐步独立表演各自的角色。
五、课堂上和课下反复练习，让多几个学生试演乌龟和兔子的角色。
六、固定在教室或舞台上走动的路线并着手制作道具。

舞台表演

　　利用小品脚本的前后顺序出场表演。"兔子跑，乌龟走"的部分最好一起朗诵。四句童谣可由小兔子们和小乌龟们分别朗诵。集体朗诵时，在台中站成半圈，独自表演的人应走到台前的中间。表演的台词要说得流利，但不要说得太快。角色多少如有不妥，可删减也可增加。

评估小结

一、看全班大部分同学是否都能把这个故事从头到尾讲下来。
二、讨论这个寓言故事的含义并与实际生活中的事情联系起来。

请上网www.cheng-tsui.com查看作者有关道具制作和选用服装的建议。也请您与大家分享您的好主意和成果。

Teaching Reference

Background Information

"The Turtle and the Hare" is a fable enjoyed by children all over the world. Here it is retold in the form of a skit in two acts. The first act occurs before the race and consists of a conversation between the turtle and the hare. The turtle and the hare each have four lines to say; these lines are similar in terms of sentence structure but different in terms of opinion.

The second act takes place during the race and is created in the form of a Total Physical Response (TPR) story. Two action verbs, "run" and "walk," carry the story to its end. The hare has more lines to say and act out than does the turtle. It can be an enjoyable classroom activity or a stage performance involving the entire class.

Teaching Suggestions

Act I involves the performers introducing themselves. Each student should be able to tell the audience who he/she is and what his/her opinion is regarding the race. Depending on the number of students in the class, students can perform this part as a class or in smaller groups.

For Act II, let students decide the type of action required to match verb phrases for "run" and "walk." It should take about two to three hours of homework for students to learn the expressions and memorize the lines. Make sure every verb phrase in the TPR story has a fixed action.

Preparatory Steps

1. Teach "run" and "walk" and four-line rhymes using TPR. For example:
   The hare runs, whizzing by. (Draw a big Z character backward to show how fast Hare runs.)
   The turtle walks slowly. (Walk with two arms moving slowly back and forth.)
2. Find out which role is best for each individual student to perform.
3. Assign roles and read participant monologues out loud.
4. Have students repeat each monologue after you, and correct their pronunciation.
5. Practice as many times as needed until students can recite the lines themselves.
6. Rotate the roles so that each student has a chance to be the Turtle or the Hare.

Stage Performance

For the monologues in Act I, individual actors should go to the front of the stage and speak slowly and clearly. Act II requires students to speak together and act with coordinated movements. Have students practice the lines "the rabbit runs and the turtle walks" while performing the actions.

Assessment:

1. See if students can retell the story in Chinese.
2. Discuss the meaning of the fable. Ask students to think of a similar situation in their own lives.

**Visit www.cheng-tsui.com for stage prop and costume suggestions by the author.
Also, share your own ideas and accomplishments!**

The Legend of Mulan

mù lán de chuán shuō
木 兰 的 传 说

This is a line-by-line rendition of the Legend of Mulan. This legend should be presented in a storytelling format, with students taking turns to say the lines. Any number of students from two to twenty-four can participate.

       mù lán shì yí ge nǚ hái zi
一、木 兰 是 一 个 女 孩 子。
Mulan was a girl.

       mù lán shí bā suì
二、木 兰 十 八 岁。
Mulan was eighteen years old.

       mù lán shì zhōng guó rén
三、木 兰 是 中 国 人。
Mulan was Chinese.

       mù lán zhù zài zhōng guó
四、木 兰 住 在 中 国。
Mulan lived in China.

       mù lán yǒu yì pǐ mǎ
五、木 兰 有 一 匹 马。
Mulan had a horse.

六、木兰有一只小狗。
mù lán yǒu yì zhī xiǎo gǒu
Mulan had a little dog.

七、木兰有木术。
mù lán yǒu mù shù
Mulan had Mushu.*

八、木术是木兰的好朋友。
mù shù shì mù lán de hǎo péng you
Mushu was Mulan's good friend.

九、木兰有一只福蝈蝈。
mù lán yǒu yì zhī fú guō guo
Mulan had a lucky cricket.

十、福蝈蝈儿很小,很可爱。
fú guō guor hěn xiǎo hěn kě ài
The lucky cricket was very small and cute.

十一、木兰喜欢福蝈蝈。
mù lán xǐ huan fú guō guo
Mulan liked the lucky cricket.

十二、木兰有爸爸,妈妈和婆婆。
mù lán yǒu bà ba mā ma hé pó po
Mulan had a father, mother, and grandmother.

*Mushu is the little dragon in the movie version of the legend.

十三、木兰没有哥哥和弟弟。
mù lán méi yǒu gē ge hé dì di
Mulan had no older brothers or younger brothers.

十四、木兰也没有姐姐和妹妹。
mù lán yě méi yǒu jiě jie hé mèi mei
Mulan had no older sisters or younger sisters either.

十五、木兰的爸爸得去打仗。
mù lán de bà ba děi qù dǎ zhàng
Mulan's father had to go fight in the war.

十六、木兰的爸爸老了。
mù lán de bà ba lǎo le
Mulan's father was getting old.

十七、木兰会骑马，会武术。
mù lán huì qí mǎ huì wǔ shù
Mulan knew how to ride a horse and perform martial arts.

十八、木兰女扮男装去打仗。
mù lán nǚ bàn nán zhuāng qù dǎ zhàng
Mulan dressed as a man and went to fight in the war.

十九、木兰很勇敢。
mù lán hěn yǒng gǎn
Mulan was very brave.

二十、木兰受伤了。
mù lán shòu shāng le
Mulan was injured.

The Legend of Mulan • 57

二十一、木兰立战功。
mù lán lì zhàn gōng

Mulan was honored in the war.

二十二、木兰要回家照看爸爸妈妈。
mù lán yào huí jiā zhào kàn bà ba mā ma

Mulan wanted to return home and take care of her parents.

二十三、木兰的假名叫"平"。
mù lán de jiǎ míng jiào píng

Mulan's fake name was Ping.

二十四、木兰是中国古代的女英雄。
mù lán shì zhōng guó gǔ dài de nǚ yīng xióng

Mulan was a heroine of ancient China.

THE END

Example of a Cross-talk Performance

(**Note to Teachers:** *In this optional cross-talk performance, four students take roles and improvise their own lines and humor while presenting the story. See the Teaching Reference pages for more ideas about cross-talk performances.*)

A: Have you ever heard the English song "Reflection" in the movie Mulan?

B: Of course, I can sing it. (*sings it with a terrible tune*)

C: Ow! My ears! Why don't you say something about Mulan in Chinese instead?

B: Okay. Mulan is 木兰 (mù lán). (*laughs*)

A: Right. Can you say, "Mulan was a girl and she lived in China"?

B: 木兰是一个女孩子，她住在中国。
(mù lán shì yí ge nǚ hái zi tā zhù zài zhōng guó)

C: Can you say, "Mulan is eighteen years old"?

B: 木兰十八岁。(mù lán shí bā suì) Why are you asking me? You do some work. Do you know the name of Mulan's good friend?

D: Do you mean the little dragon in the movie? It is 木术 (mù shù).

B: Say it in Chinese. "Mushu is Mulan's good friend."

D: 木术是木兰的好朋友。
(mù shù shì mù lán de hǎo péng yǒu)

C: How about "Mulan had a lucky cricket"?

D: 木兰有一只福蝈蝈。
(mù lán yǒu yì zhī fú guō guo)

A: Say, "The lucky cricket is small and cute."

D: 福蝈蝈很小，很可爱。
(fú guō guo hěn xiǎo hěn kě ài)
See, it's easy. I have an easy one for you to try: "Mulan has a mom, dad and grandmother."

The Legend of Mulan

C: mù lán yǒu bà ba mā ma hé pó po
木兰有爸爸,妈妈和婆婆。
Give me something more difficult.

A: Okay. "Mulan's father is old."

C: mù lán de lǎo bà
木兰的老爸。 Why do I always get the hard questions?

A: I can tell that you don't know the answer to this question. You should say:

mù lán de bà ba lǎo le
木兰的爸爸老了。

C: Not that much difference. bà lǎo lǎo bà 爸老,老爸。 Same thing.

A: No, it isn't. Let me give you an easy one: "Mulan doesn't have any brothers."

C: No problem: mù lán méi yǒu gē ge hé dì di 木兰没有哥哥和弟弟。

D: That's an easy one, too. How about: "Mulan knows how to ride a horse and how to perform martial arts."

C: mù lán huì qí mǎ mù lán huì wǔ shù
木兰会骑马,木兰会武术。 Now it's my turn. (*say to B*) I'll bet you can't say: "Mulan pretended to be a man and went to fight."

B: mù lán nǚ bàn nán zhuāng qù dǎ zhàng
木兰女扮男装去打仗。

(*say to A*) It's your turn now.

C: (*say to A*) How about you say: "Mulan was very brave."

A: Try me: mù lán hěn yǒng gǎn 木兰很勇敢。 (*with great confidence*)

B: Mulan was honored after the war.

A: mù lán lì zhàn gōng
木兰立战功。

C: Mulan was injured.

A: mù lán shòu shāng le
木兰受伤了。

D: Mulan did not want to be a high-ranking official. How about you say: "she wanted to return home and take care of her parents?"

A:
mù lán yào huí jiā zhào kàn bà ba mā ma
木兰要回家照看爸爸妈妈。

B: Mulan's fake name was Ping.

A:
mù lán de jiǎ míng jiào píng
木兰的假名叫"平"。

ABCD: Mulan was a heroine of ancient China.

mù lán shì zhōng guó gǔ dài de nǚ yīng xióng
木兰是中国古代的女英雄。

xiè xie
谢谢。 *(bow to audience)*

Note: Create your own cross-talk and make it funny and entertaining.

The Legend of Mulan • 61

教学参考

背景介绍

"木兰的传说"是根据木兰的传说改写的。为了便于初学汉语的学生能利用木兰的故事学汉语，改编的内容是由一句一句的最简单的句子组成的。用意在句子上，不在故事上。为了增加趣味，还加进了相声表演的形式。

教学建议

这个故事可以有两种表演方法。一种是简单地讲故事，另一种是相声形式的即兴表演。

简单地讲故事可以由一个学生表演，也可以由几个学生一起表演。学演的过程中，应注重语音语调的提高。

相声的表演需要四个学生做即兴的问答。木兰故事中的二十四句话，在四个学生的英语对话中被再次讲述，有些句子还可以发挥。总的意思是学生们互相挑战看对方是否可以用中文讲木兰的故事。相声表演练习的大部分时间应用课下时间来完成。

具体步骤

一、用木兰的故事复习已学过的句型。如："木兰住在中国"和"木兰没有哥哥和弟弟"等。
二、用替换练习的方法学"得"和"要"的句型。如："我得睡觉"，"他得吃饭"和"我要回家"等。
三、从故事的情节中介绍新词汇，如："女扮男装"和"去打仗"等。
四、用一人一句讲故事的方法熟悉木兰的二十四个句子。
五、给一周的时间让学生消化、记忆和背诵句子。

舞台表演

如果上台表演一人一句讲木兰的故事，三个学生表演效果较好。如果观众不懂中文，应先用英语说明意思，再说中文句子。一板一眼慢慢地讲。相声的部分较适合五、六年级以上的学生。相声的幽默滑稽多在于学生的表达能力和性格，注意挑适当人选。

评估小结

一、学生有能力用简单的句子叙述木兰的故事。
二、学生有能力用简单的句子描述自己或是他人。

请上网 www.cheng-tsui.com 查看作者有关道具制作和选用服装的建议。也请您与大家分享您的好主意和成果。

Teaching Reference

Background Information

This play was inspired by the traditional Chinese legend Mulan. With its short length of only twenty-four lines and its use of repetition, the play serves as an opportunity for students to review basic sentence structure and vocabulary. Younger students can tell the story directly from the script, while older, more advanced students can be challenged to use "cross-talk" to make a humorous, creative presentation.

Teaching Suggestions

This story can be presented in two ways: a simple storytelling presentation or a cross-talk presentation with student improvisation.

A simple storytelling presentation can be performed either by one student or by a group of students taking turns to tell the story. Accurate pronunciation and intonation should be emphasized in the learning process.

A cross-talk presentation involving improvisation can be performed with a group of four students. The twenty-four lines of the Mulan story will be retold through the four students' English conversation, some of which is improvised. The basic idea is that students challenge each other to say a sentence in Chinese about Mulan.

Preparatory Steps

1. Use the Mulan story to review familiar sentence structure. For example: Mulan lived in China. Mulan had no brothers.
2. Use pattern drills to teach "dei" and "yao". For example: I have to go to bed. I want to go home.
3. Introduce new phrases in the context of the story. For example: Mulan pretended to be a man. Mulan went to war.
4. Use a "one student, one sentence" method to tell the whole story.
5. Allow a week for students to learn the story and memorize their lines.

Stage Performance

For best results, three students should perform the simple storytelling version of Mulan, and four students should perform the cross-talk version. If the audience is not familiar with Chinese, presenters should speak in English first, then present the Chinese translation. The success of the cross-talk performance depends upon the humor and personality of the students. Choose students who are outgoing and eager to participate.

Assessment

1. Students are able to retell the story using their own words.
2. Students are able to say a basic sentence to describe themselves or another person.

Visit www.cheng-tsui.com for stage prop and costume suggestions by the author.
Also, share your own ideas and accomplishments!

THE TURNIP IS BACK

luó bo huí lái le
萝 卜 回 来 了

rén wù
人 物
Characters

jiě shuō yuán
解 说 员
Narrator

liǎng zhī xiǎo hóu zi
两 只 小 猴 子
Two Little Monkeys

liǎng zhī xiǎo yáng
两 只 小 羊
Two Little Goats

liǎng pǐ xiǎo mǎ
两 匹 小 马
Two Little Horses

liǎng zhī xiǎo xióng
两 只 小 熊
Two Little Bears

liǎng zhī xiǎo sōng shǔ
两 只 小 松 鼠
Two Little Squirrels

liǎng zhī xiǎo tù zi
两 只 小 兔 子
Two Little Rabbits

Season: Winter, then early Spring   **Place:** Deep in a forest

Act 1 — At the Rabbits' House

jiě shuō yuán:
解说员:
Narrator:

xià dà xuě le sēn lín shēn chù
下大雪了，森林深处
It is snowing hard. Deep in the forest,

yí piàn bái máng máng de
一片白茫茫的。
a blanket of white covers everything.

xiǎo dòng wù men jǐ tiān méi yǒu
小动物们几天没有
Little creatures have not

chū lái zhǎo chī de dōng xi le
出来找吃的东西了，
come out for days to look for food,

tā men dōu hěn è
他们都很饿。
and they are very hungry.

(both Rabbits stand up and start to stretch their arms)

xiǎo tù zi yī:
小兔子一:
Little Rabbit 1:

gē ge wǒ zhēn è
哥哥，我真饿。
Big Brother, I'm starving.

nǐ è ma
你饿吗？
Are you hungry?

xiǎo tù zi èr: wǒ yě hěn è
小兔子二: 我也很饿。
Little Rabbit 2: I'm very hungry, too.

wǒ men yǒu liǎng ge luó bo
我们有两个萝卜。
We have two turnips.

wǒ men chī luó bó ba
我们吃萝卜吧。
Let's eat them.

xiǎo tù zi yī: hǎo wǒ xǐ huan chī luó bo
小兔子一: 好。我喜欢吃萝卜。
Little Rabbit 1: Good. I like to eat turnips.

nǐ chī yí ge wǒ chī yí ge
你吃一个,我吃一个。
You eat one and I'll eat one.

xiǎo tù zi èr: dì di wǒ men chī yí ge
小兔子二: 弟弟,我们吃一个
Little Rabbit 2: Little Brother, let's just eat one

luó bo hǎo ma
萝卜,好吗?
turnip, okay?

xiǎo tù zi yī: wèi shén me
小兔子一: 为什么?
Little Rabbit 1: Why?

小兔子二:
Little Rabbit 2:

xiǎo yáng yí dìng hěn è
小羊一定很饿。
The Little Goats must be starving.

yí ge luó bo gěi xiǎo yáng
一个萝卜给小羊,
Let's give one turnip to the Little Goats,

hǎo bù hǎo
好不好?
okay?

小兔子一:
Little Rabbit 1:

hǎo ba   yí ge luó bo gěi xiǎo yáng
好吧!一个萝卜给小羊。
All right! We will give one turnip to Little Goat.
(*they walk to the Little Goats' house*)

小兔子二:
Little Rabbit 2:

zhè shì xiǎo yáng de jiā
这是小羊的家。
This is the Little Goats' home. (*they knock on the door*)

小兔子一:
Little Rabbit 1:

méi yǒu rén
没有人。
Nobody is home.

兔子一二:
Little Rabbits 1 & 2:

liú xià luó bo gěi xiǎo yáng
留下萝卜给小羊。
Leave the turnip for the Little Goats.

wǒ men zài qù zhǎo
我们再去找。
We will go to look for something else. (*they exit*)

Act 2   At the Goats' House

(both Little Goats stand up and stretch their arms)

xiǎo yáng yī: / 小羊一: / Little Goat 1:
jiě jie wǒ zhēn è nǐ è ma
姐姐，我真饿。你饿吗？
Big Sister, I'm starving. Are you hungry?

xiǎo yáng èr: / 小羊二: / Little Goat 2:
wǒ yě hěn è wǒ men qù zhǎo
我也很饿。我们去找
I'm really hungry, too. Let's go to look for

chī de dōng xi ba
吃的东西吧。
something to eat.

xiǎo yáng yī: / 小羊一: / Little Goat 1:
hǎo a jiě jie jiě jie
好啊。姐姐，姐姐，
All right. Big Sister, Big Sister,

nǐ kàn zhè shì shén me
你看，这是什么？
look, what is this?

xiǎo yáng èr: / 小羊二: / Little Goat 2:
zhè shì luó bo yí ge dà luó bo
这是萝卜，一个大萝卜。
It is a turnip, a big turnip.

xiǎo yáng yī: / 小羊一: / Little Goat 1:
wǒ xǐ huan chī luó bo
我喜欢吃萝卜。
I like to eat turnips.

xiǎo yáng èr: wǒ yě xǐ huan chī luó bo
小羊二: 我也喜欢吃萝卜。
Little Goat 2: I also like to eat turnips.

xiǎo yáng yī: zhè shì shéi de luó bo
小羊一: 这是谁的萝卜?
Little Goat 1: Whose turnip is it?

xiǎo yáng èr: wǒ bù zhī dào
小羊二: 我不知道。
Little Goat 2: I don't know.

xiǎo yáng yī: zhè bú shì wǒ men de luó bo
小羊一: 这不是我们的萝卜。
Little Goat 1: This is not our turnip.

xiǎo yáng èr: xiǎo hóu zi yí dìng hěn è
小羊二: 小猴子一定很饿。
Little Goat 2: The Little Monkeys must be starving.

luó bo gěi xiǎo hóu zi
萝卜给小猴子,
Let's give the turnip to the Little Monkeys,

hǎo bù hǎo
好不好?
okay?

xiǎo yáng yī: hǎo a luó bo gěi xiǎo hóu zi
小羊一: 好啊, 萝卜给小猴子。
Little Goat 1: Okay. We'll give the turnip to the Little Monkeys.

xiǎo yáng èr: zhè shì xiǎo hóu zi de jiā
小羊二: 这是小猴子的家。
Little Goat 2: This is the Little Monkeys' home. (*knocks on the door*)

xiǎoyáng yī:
小 羊 一：

Little Goat 1:

méi yǒu rén
没 有 人。

No one is home.

xiǎo yáng yī èr:
小 羊 一 二：

Little Goats 1 & 2:

liú xià luó bo gěi xiǎo hóu zi
留 下 萝 卜 给 小 猴 子。

Let's leave the turnip for the Little Monkeys.

wǒ men zài qù zhǎo
我 们 再 去 找。

We will go and find something else. (*Little Goats exit*)

Act 3   At the Monkeys' House

(*both Little Monkeys are yawning and stretching*)

hóu zi yī:
猴 子 一：

Little Monkey 1:

gē ge wǒ zhēn è
哥 哥，我 真 饿。

Big Brother, I'm starving.

nǐ è ma
你 饿 吗？

Are you hungry?

hóu zi èr:
猴 子 二：

Little Monkey 2:

wǒ yě hěn è wǒ men qù
我 也 很 饿。我 们 去

I'm very hungry, too. Let's go

zhǎo chī de dōng xi ba
找 吃 的 东 西 吧。

to find something to eat.

The Turnip Is Back • 71

猴子一 / Little Monkey 1: 好啊。哥哥，哥哥，
hǎo a gē ge gē ge
Okay. Big Brother, Big Brother,

你看，这是什么？
nǐ kàn zhè shì shén me
look, what is this?

猴子二 / Little Monkey 2: 这是萝卜，一个大萝卜。
zhè shì luó bo yí ge dà luó bo
This is a turnip, a big turnip.

猴子一 / Little Monkey 1: 我喜欢吃萝卜。
wǒ xǐ huan chī luó bo
I like to eat turnips.

猴子二 / Little Monkey 2: 我也喜欢吃萝卜。
wǒ yě xǐ huan chī luó bo
I like to eat turnips, too.

猴子一 / Little Monkey 1: 这是谁的萝卜？
zhè shì shéi de luó bo
Whose turnip is it?

猴子二 / Little Monkey 2: 我不知道。
wǒ bù zhī dào
I don't know.

猴子一 / Little Monkey 1: 这不是我们的萝卜。
zhè bú shì wǒ men de luó bo
This is not our turnip.

猴子二 / Little Monkey 2: 小马一定很饿。
xiǎo mǎ yí dìng hěn è
The Little Horses must be starving.

luó bo gěi xiǎo mǎ
萝卜给小马,
Let's give the turnip to the Little Horses,

hǎo bù hǎo
好不好?
okay?

hóu zi yī:
猴子一:
Little Monkey 1:

hǎo a luó bo gěi xiǎo mǎ
好啊。萝卜给小马。
All right. Give the turnip to the Little Horses.

hóu zi èr:
猴子二:
Little Monkey 2:

zhè shì xiǎo mǎ de jiā
这是小马的家。
This is the Little Horses' home. (knocks on the door)

hóu zi yī:
猴子一:
Little Monkey 1:

méi yǒu rén
没有人。
No one is home.

hóu zi yī èr:
猴子一二:
Little Monkeys 1 & 2:

liú xià luó bo gěi xiǎo mǎ
留下萝卜给小马。
Let's leave the turnip for the Little Horses.

wǒ men zài qù zhǎo
我们再去找。
We will go and find something else. (they exit)

The Turnip Is Back • 73

Act 4 — At the Horses' House

(both Little Horses are stretching and yawning)

xiǎo mǎ yī: 小 马 一: Little Horse 1:	jiě jie wǒ zhēn è nǐ è ma 姐 姐, 我 真 饿。你 饿 吗? Big Sister, I'm starving. Are you hungry?
xiǎo mǎ èr: 小 马 二: Little Horse 2:	wǒ yě hěn è wǒ men qù zhǎo 我 也 很 饿。我 们 去 找 I'm very hungry, too. Let's go out to chī de dōng xi ba 吃 的 东 西 吧。 find something to eat.
xiǎo mǎ yī: 小 马 一: Little Horse 1:	hǎo a jiě jie jiě jie 好 啊。姐 姐, 姐 姐, All right. Big Sister, Big Sister, nǐ kàn zhè shì shén me 你 看, 这 是 什 么? look, what is this?
xiǎo mǎ èr: 小 马 二: Little Horse 2:	zhè shì luó bo yí ge dà luó bo 这 是 萝 卜, 一 个 大 萝 卜。 This is a turnip, a big turnip.
xiǎo mǎ yī: 小 马 一: Little Horse 1:	wǒ xǐ huan chī luó bo 我 喜 欢 吃 萝 卜。 I like to eat turnips.
xiǎo mǎ èr: 小 马 二: Little Horse 2:	wǒ yě xǐ huan chī luó bo 我 也 喜 欢 吃 萝 卜。 I also like to eat turnips.

xiǎo mǎ yī: zhè shì shéi de luó bo
小马一： 这是谁的萝卜？
Little Horse 1: Whose turnip is it?

xiǎo mǎ èr: wǒ bù zhī dào
小马二： 我不知道。
Little Horse 2: I don't know.

xiǎo mǎ yī: zhè bú shì wǒ men de luó bo
小马一： 这不是我们的萝卜。
Little Horse 1: This is not our turnip. (shakes his/her head)

xiǎo mǎ èr: xiǎo xióng yí dìng hěn è
小马二： 小熊一定很饿。
Little Horse 2: The Little Bears must be starving.

luó bo gěi xiǎo xióng hǎo bù hǎo
萝卜给小熊，好不好？
Let's give the turnip to the Little Bears, is that all right?

xiǎo mǎ yī: hǎo a luó bo gěi xiǎo xióng
小马一： 好啊。萝卜给小熊。
Little Horse 1: All right. We'll give the turnip to the Little Bears.

(both Little Horses walk down to the Little Bears' house)

xiǎo mǎ èr: zhè shì xiǎo xióng de jiā
小马二： 这是小熊的家。
Little Horse 2: This is the Little Bears' home. (knocks on the door)

xiǎo mǎ yī: méi yǒu rén
小马一： 没有人。
Little Horse 1: Nobody answers.

The Turnip Is Back • 75

xiǎo mǎ yī èr:
小 马 一 二：
Little Horses 1 & 2:

liú xià luó bo gěi xiǎo xióng
留 下 萝 卜 给 小 熊。
Let's leave the turnip for the Little Bears.

wǒ men zài qù zhǎo
我 们 再 去 找。
We will go to find something else. (*they exit*)

Act 5 At the Bears' House

(*both Little Bears stand up and start to stretch*)

xiǎo xióng yī:
小 熊 一：
Little Bear 1:

gē ge wǒ zhēn è
哥 哥，我 真 饿。
Big Brother, I'm starving.

nǐ è ma
你 饿 吗？
Are you hungry?

xiǎo xióng èr:
小 熊 二：
Little Bear 2:

wǒ yě hěn è wǒ men qù
我 也 很 饿。我 们 去
I'm very hungry, too. Let's go to

zhǎo chī de dōng xi ba
找 吃 的 东 西 吧。
find something to eat.

xiǎo xióng yī: 小 熊 一: Little Bear 1:	hǎo a gē ge gē ge 好 啊。哥 哥,哥 哥, All right. Big Brother, Big Brother,	

nǐ kàn zhè shì shén me
你 看,这 是 什 么?
look, what is this?

xiǎo xióng èr:
小 熊 二:
Little Bear 2:

zhè shì luó bo
这 是 萝 卜,
This is a turnip,

yí ge dà luó bo
一 个 大 萝 卜。
a big turnip.

xiǎo xióng yī:
小 熊 一:
Little Bear 1:

wǒ xǐ huan chī luó bo
我 喜 欢 吃 萝 卜。
I like to eat turnips.

xiǎo xióng èr:
小 熊 二:
Little Bear 2:

wǒ yě xǐ huan chī luó bo
我 也 喜 欢 吃 萝 卜。
I like to eat turnips, too.

xiǎo xióng yī:
小 熊 一:
Little Bear 1:

zhè shì shéi de luó bo
这 是 谁 的 萝 卜?
Whose turnip is it?

xiǎo xióng èr:
小 熊 二:
Little Bear 2:

wǒ bù zhī dào
我 不 知 道。
I don't know.

小熊一: 这不是我们的萝卜。
Little Bear 1: This is not our turnip. (*disappointed*)

小熊二: 小松鼠一定很饿。
Little Bear 2: The Little Squirrels must be starving.

萝卜给小松鼠,
Let's give the turnip to the Little Squirrels,

好不好?
is that all right?

小熊一: 好啊。萝卜给
Little Bear 1: Fine. We will give the turnip to the

小松鼠。
Little Squirrels.

小熊二: 这是小松鼠的家。
Little Bear 2: This is the Little Squirrels' home. (*knocks on the door*)

小熊一: 没有人。
Little Bear 1: No one answers.

xiǎo xióng yī èr: 小 熊 一 二： **Little Bears 1 & 2:**	liú xià luó bo gěi xiǎo sōng shǔ 留 下 萝 卜 给 小 松 鼠。 Let's leave the turnip for the Little Squirrels.
	wǒ men zài qù zhǎo 我 们 再 去 找。 We will go to find something else. *(they exit)*

Act 6 — In Early Spring

(little animals follow narrator's words, return to stage with props and sit down behind their own houses)

jiě shuō yuán: 解 说 员： **Narrator:**	xiǎo yáng zhǎo dào qīng cǎo 小 羊 找 到 青 草。 The Little Goats have found green grass.
	xiǎo hóu zi zhǎo dào huā shēng 小 猴 子 找 到 花 生。 The Little Monkeys have found peanuts.
	xiǎo xióng zhǎo dào yù mǐ 小 熊 找 到 玉 米。 The Little Bears have found corn.
	xiǎo mǎ zhǎo dào qīng cǎo 小 马 找 到 青 草。 The Little Horses have found green grass.
	xiǎo tù zi zhǎo dào hú luó bo 小 兔 子 找 到 胡 萝 卜。 The Little Rabbits have found carrots.

nà me xiǎo sōng shū
那么，小 松 鼠
So, have the Little Squirrels

yǒu méi yǒu zhǎo dào shén me
有 没 有 找 到 什 么
found anything

chī de dōng xi ne
吃 的 东 西 呢？
to eat yet?

(two Little Squirrels slowly stand up, yawning and stretching)

sōng shǔ yī: jiě jie wǒ zhēn è nǐ è ma
松 鼠 一：   姐 姐，我 真 饿。你 饿 吗？
Little Squirrel 1:   Big Sister, I'm starving. Are you hungry?

sōng shǔ èr: wǒ yě hěn è wǒ men qù zhǎo
松 鼠 二：   我 也 很 饿。我 们 去 找
Little Squirrel 2:   I'm also very hungry. Let's go to find

chī de dōng xi ba
吃 的 东 西 吧。
something to eat.

sōng shǔ yī: hǎo a jiě jie jiě jie nǐ kàn
松 鼠 一：   好 啊。姐 姐，姐 姐，你 看，
Little Squirrel 1:   All right. Big Sister, Big Sister, look,

zhè shì shén me
这 是 什 么？
what is this?

sōng shǔ èr: zhè shì luó bo yí ge dà luó bo
松 鼠 二：   这 是 萝 卜，一 个 大 萝 卜。
Little Squirrel 2:   It is a turnip, a big turnip.

sōng shǔ yī: wǒ xǐ huan chī luó bo
松鼠一： 我喜欢吃萝卜。
Little Squirrel 1: I like to eat turnips.

sōng shǔ èr: wǒ yě xǐ huan chī luó bo
松鼠二： 我也喜欢吃萝卜。
Little Squirrel 2: I also like to eat turnips.

sōng shǔ yī: zhè shì shéi de luó bo
松鼠一： 这是谁的萝卜？
Little Squirrel 1: Whose turnip is it?

sōng shǔ èr: wǒ bù zhī dào
松鼠二： 我不知道。
Little Squirrel 2: I don't know.

sōng shǔ yī: zhè bú shì wǒ men de luó bo
松鼠一： 这不是我们的萝卜。
Little Squirrel 1: This is not our turnip.

sōng shǔ èr: xiǎo xióng yí dìng hěn è
松鼠二： 小熊一定很饿。
Little Squirrel 2: The Little Bears must be starving.

luó bo gěi xiǎo xióng hǎo bù hǎo
萝卜给小熊，好不好？
Let's give the turnip to the Little Bears, okay?

sōng shǔ yī: hǎo a luó bo gěi xiǎo xióng
松鼠一： 好啊。萝卜给小熊。
Little Squirrel 1: Okay. We'll give the turnip to the Little Bears.

(two Squirrels walk towards the Little Bears' home)

sōng shǔ èr: zhè shì xiǎo xióng de jiā
松鼠二： 这是小熊的家。
Little Squirrel 2: This is the Little Bears' home. *(knocks on the door)*

小熊一: 谁呀？
Little Bear 1: Who is it?

松鼠一: 是我。
Little Squirrel 1: It's me.

小熊二: 你是谁？
Little Bear 2: Who are you?

松鼠二: 我们是小松鼠。
Little Squirrel 2: We are Little Squirrels.

小熊一: 请进。欢迎，欢迎。
Little Bear 1: Please come in. Welcome.

松鼠一: 请问，这是你们的萝卜吗？
Little Squirrel 1: May I ask if this turnip is yours? (*holds up the turnip*)

小熊二: 不是。
Little Bear 2: No, it is not.

松鼠二: 这是谁的萝卜？
Little Squirrel 2: Whose turnip is it?

wǒ men qù wèn yí wèn
我们去问一问，
Let's go ask around,

hǎo bù hǎo
好不好？
shall we?

xiǎo xióng yī: hǎo a
小 熊 一： 好啊。
Little Bear 1: All right.

(together they walk down to the Little Horses' home)

sōng shǔ yī: zhè shì xiǎo mǎ de jiā
松 鼠 一： 这是小马的家。
Little Squirrel 1: This is the Little Horses' home. *(knocks on the door)*

xiǎo mǎ yī: shéi yā
小 马 一： 谁呀？
Little Horse 1: Who is it?

sōng shǔ èr: shì wǒ
松 鼠 二： 是我。
Little Squirrel 2: It's me.

xiǎo mǎ èr: nǐ shì shéi
小 马 二： 你是谁？
Little Horse 2: Who are you?

sōng shǔ yī: wǒ men shì xiǎo sōng shǔ
松 鼠 一： 我们是小松鼠。
Little Squirrel 1: We are Little Squirrels.

xiǎo mǎ yī: qǐng jìn huān yíng huān yíng
小 马 一： 请进。欢迎，欢迎。
Little Horse 1: Please come in. Welcome.

The Turnip Is Back • **83**

松鼠二 (sōng shǔ èr):
Little Squirrel 2:

请问，这是你们的萝卜吗？
qǐng wèn, zhè shì nǐ men de luó bo ma
May I ask if this is your turnip? (*holds up the turnip*)

小马二 (xiǎo mǎ èr):
Little Horse 2:

不是。
bú shì
No, it is not.

松鼠一 (sōng shǔ yī):
Little Squirrel 1:

这是谁的萝卜？
zhè shì shéi de luó bo
Whose turnip is it?

我们去问一问，
wǒ men qù wèn yí wèn
Let's go ask around,

好不好？
hǎo bù hǎo
shall we?

小马和小熊 (xiǎo mǎ hé xiǎo xióng):
Little Horses and Little Bears:

好吧！
hǎo ba
All right! (*walk down to the Little Monkeys' home*)

小熊二 (xiǎo xióng èr):
Little Bear 2:

这是小猴子的家。
zhè shì xiǎo hóu zi de jiā
This is the Little Monkeys' home. (*knocks on the door*)

猴子一 (hóu zi yī):
Little Monkey 1:

谁呀？
shéi yā
Who is it?

xiǎo xióng yī: 小 熊 一： Little Bear 1:	shì wǒ 是 我。 It's me.
hóu zi èr: 猴 子 二： Little Monkey 2:	nǐ shì shéi 你 是 谁？ Who are you?
xiǎo xióng èr: 小 熊 二： Little Bear 2:	wǒ men shì xiǎo xióng 我 们 是 小 熊。 We are Little Bears.
hóu zi yī: 猴 子 一： Little Monkey 1:	qǐng jìn huān yíng huān yíng 请 进。欢 迎，欢 迎。 Please come in. Welcome.
xiǎo xióng yī: 小 熊 一： Little Bear 1:	qǐng wèn zhè shì nǐ men de 请 问，这 是 你 们 的 May I ask if this is your luó bo ma 萝 卜 吗？ turnip? (*holds up the turnip*)
hóu zi èr: 猴 子 二： Little Monkey 2:	bú shì 不 是。 No, it is not. (*shakes head*)
xiǎo xióng èr: 小 熊 二： Little Bear 2:	zhè shì shéi de luó bo 这 是 谁 的 萝 卜？ Whose turnip is it? wǒ men qù wèn yí wèn 我 们 去 问 一 问， Let's go ask around,

	hǎo bù hǎo
	好 不 好？
	shall we?

hóu zi xiǎo mǎ	
猴子、小马	
Little Monkeys, Horses	

hé sōng shǔ:	hǎo ba
和 松 鼠：	好 吧！
and Squirrels:	Okay!

(little animals walk down to the Little Goats' home)

xiǎo mǎ yī:	zhè shì xiǎo yáng de jiā
小 马 一：	这 是 小 羊 的 家。
Little Horse 1:	This is the Little Goats' home. *(knocks on the door)*

xiǎo yáng yī:	shéi yā
小 羊 一：	谁 呀？
Little Goat 1:	Who is it?

xiǎo mǎ èr:	shì wǒ
小 马 二：	是 我。
Little Horse 2:	It's me.

xiǎo yáng èr:	nǐ shì shéi
小 羊 二：	你 是 谁？
Little Goat 2:	Who are you?

xiǎo mǎ yī:	wǒ men shì xiǎo mǎ
小 马 一：	我 们 是 小 马。
Little Horse 1:	We are Little Horses.

小羊一 (xiǎo yáng yī) / Little Goat 1:
请进。欢迎，欢迎。
(qǐng jìn. huān yíng, huān yíng.)
Please come in. Welcome.

小马二 (xiǎo mǎ èr) / Little Horse 2:
请问，这是你们的萝卜吗？
(qǐng wèn, zhè shì nǐ men de luó bo ma)
May I ask if this is your turnip? (*holds up the turnip*)

小羊二 (xiǎo yáng èr) / Little Goat 2:
不是。
(bú shì.)
No, it is not.

小马一 (xiǎo mǎ yī) / Little Horse 1:
这是谁的萝卜？
(zhè shì shéi de luó bo)
Whose turnip is it?

我们去问一问，
(wǒ men qù wèn yí wèn,)
Let's go ask around,

好不好？
(hǎo bù hǎo)
shall we?

小羊、小熊、猴子和松鼠 (xiǎo yáng, xiǎo xióng, hóu zi hé sōng shǔ) / Little Goats, Little Bears, Little Monkeys, and Little Squirrels:
好吧！
(hǎo ba)
Okay! (*actors walk down to the Little Rabbits' home*)

The Turnip Is Back

猴子一: 这是小兔子的家。
Little Monkey 1: This is the Little Rabbits' home. (*knocks on the door*)

兔子一: 谁呀?
Little Rabbit 1: Who is it?

猴子二: 是我。
Little Monkey 1: It's me.

兔子二: 你是谁?
Little Rabbit 2: Who are you?

猴子一: 我们是小猴子。
Little Monkey 1: We are Little Monkeys.

兔子一: 请进。欢迎,欢迎。
Little Rabbit 1: Please come in. Welcome.

猴子二: 请问,这是你们的萝卜吗?
Little Monkey 2: May I ask if this is your turnip?

兔子二: (tù zi èr)
让我看一看。是，这是我们的萝卜。
(ràng wǒ kàn yí kàn. shì, zhè shì wǒ men de luó bo)
Little Rabbit 2: Let me take a look. Yes, this is our turnip. (*surprised*)

大家: (dà jiā)
这是小兔子的萝卜。
(zhè shì xiǎo tù zi de luó bo)
All: This is the Little Rabbits' turnip. (*happily*)

兔子一: (tù zi yī)
萝卜怎么回来了？
(luó bo zěn me huí lái le)
Little Rabbit 1: How did the turnip get back here? (*very surprised*)

大家: (dà jiā)
萝卜回来了！
萝卜回来了！
(luó bo huí lái le)
All: The turnip is back! The turnip is back! (*clapping hands*)

兔子二: (tù zi èr)
我们一起吃萝卜，好吗？
(wǒ men yì qǐ chī luó bo, hǎo ma)
Little Rabbit 2: Let's eat the turnip together, shall we?

大家: (dà jiā)
好，谢谢。
(hǎo xiè xie)
Everyone: All right! Thank you.

The Turnip Is Back

wǒ men dà jiā yì qǐ chī luó bo
我们大家一起吃萝卜。
Let's all eat the turnip together.
(all the animals pretend to eat turnip and then quickly return to their homes)

jiě shuō yuán: zhè shì wǒ men de gù shi
解说员: 这是我们的故事,
Narrator: This is our story,

luó bo huí lái le
"萝卜回来了"。
"The Turnip Is Back."

nǐ xǐ huan ma
你喜欢吗?
Did you like it?

(performers take turns standing up to say the following lines)

wǒ shì
我是 ...
I am... *(say your real name)*.

wǒ bàn yǎn
我扮演 ...
I play the part of... *(say your role)*.

xiè xie zài jiàn
谢谢。再见。
All: Thank you. Goodbye.

THE END

教学参考

背景介绍

"萝卜回来了"的故事是中国最著名的童话故事之一。这个小品是根据这个童话故事而改编的。改编的故事全部都是用对话形式的问答句,为学生提供一个练习基本语言功能的机会。故事从两只小兔子的对话开始,到五对其他小动物们之间的对话。对话结束了故事也讲完了。虽然每个角色的对话内容大致相同,可是萝卜是怎么回来的讲得很清楚。学生们喜欢各自的角色并受益于反复聆听其他同学的台词。

教学建议

学过汉语一年的学生们应该能够表演这个小品。小品中角色的多少,可以根据各自班上的学生的人数来调整。一般情况下,让学生自己找搭档。如果学生需要帮助,让能力较强的学生带另一个学生,当小先生,效果会很好。学演这个小品,大约需要五个课时和五个家庭作业的时间来完成。这个故事小品是年终结业汇报演出的好题材。

具体步骤

一、发给学生小品的脚本并根据班上人数情况做调整。
二、学生挑选角色并大声朗读各自的台词。
三、课上及时纠正语音语调并留回家朗读台词的作业。
四、学生造房子的同时老师逐个检查每对角色的对话是否正确。
五、安排朗读背诵的家庭作业并给学生足够的时间理解消化故事内容。
六、全班过小品脚本并鼓励学生提表演方面的建议。
七、固定道具(小动物的房子)的位置并反复练习台词和固定如何在舞台上走动的路线。

舞台表演

学生在教室里练习的时候,道具所放的位置应该和舞台表演时道具的位置大致相同。学生在熟悉台词的情况下,要练习并固定从一个小动物家到另一个小动物家的路线。背诵台词时,注意不要背对观众。具体的动作和小的道具的使用写在小品脚本的字里行间。表演这个小品大约需要七分钟的时间。

评估小结

一、讨论"萝卜回来了"的故事告诉了我们什么。
二、学生表演对话是否流畅自然。
三、学生是否能在类似的场合里使用小品中所学的对话。

请上网 www.cheng-tsui.com 查看作者有关道具制作和选用服装的建议。也请您与大家分享您的好主意和成果。

Teaching Reference

Background Information

The story "The Turnip Is Back" is one of the most popular fairy tales in China.

This skit is based on the fairy tale and is designed for students to practice basic greetings and short conversations. Dialogues between two little rabbits and five other pairs of little creatures are featured throughout the skit. Each pair of little creatures has a chance to ask and answer questions about "Whose turnip is this?" and the story ends with the turnip returning to the original owners' home. Students enjoy their own roles and benefit by hearing others recite familiar lines.

Teaching Suggestions

Students with one year of Chinese language learning experience should be comfortable playing a role in the skit. The number of roles in the skits depends on the number of students. The students can choose their own partners. If a student needs help, he/she should be paired with a more experienced student. About five teaching hours and five homework hours will be needed for students to recite their lines fluently and have the confidence to stand up and perform. The skit is an effective learning tool when performed as a year-end class project.

Teaching Steps

1. Adjust the number of small animals in the skit as needed.
2. Choose roles and read the script in and out of class.
3. Correct students' pronunciation and have students memorize their parts.
4. Let students build their homes while the teacher checks each pairs' progress learning their lines.
5. Allow enough time for students to understand the whole script.
6. Go over the script and encourage suggestions from students to add to the basic dialogues.
7. Set up each animal home's location and practice the whole skit.

Stage Performance

While students are practicing this skit in the classroom, the props (houses) should be arranged in the same way as they will appear on stage. Students should practice their stage route by walking from one house to the next. When students recite their lines, they should face the audience. Some stage directions are written between the lines of the script, and the performance is about seven minutes long.

Assessment

1. Describe and discuss the moral teachings of the story.
2. Evaluate student dialogues in terms of speaking fluency.
3. Determine if students can ask and answer questions in similar situations using the patterns presented in the dialogues.

Visit www.cheng-tsui.com for stage prop and costume suggestions by the author.
Also, share your own ideas and accomplishments!

Mimi Says

mī mī shuō
咪 咪 说

jiǎ: mī mī shuō
甲: 咪 咪 说,
A: Mimi says,

yǐ: shuō shén me
乙: 说 什 么?
B: Says what?

jiǎ: zhǐ zhǐ nǐ de bí zi
甲: 指 指 你 的 鼻 子。
A: Point to your nose.

yǐ: bí zi
乙: 鼻 子
B: Nose.

jiǎ: mī mī shuō
甲: 咪 咪 说,
A: Mimi says,

yǐ: shuō shén me
乙: 说 什 么?
B: Says what?

甲: 指指你的眼睛。
A: Point to your eyes.

乙: 眼睛。
B: Eyes.

甲: 咪咪说,
A: Mimi says,

乙: 说什么?
B: Says what?

甲: 指指你的嘴巴。
A: Point to your mouth.

乙: 嘴巴。
B: Mouth.

甲: 咪咪说,
A: Mimi says,

乙: 说什么?
B: Says what?

甲: 指指你的耳朵。
A: Point to your ear.

yǐ:	ěr	duo	
乙:	耳	朵。	
B:	Ear.		

jiǎ:	mī	mī	shuō
甲:	咪	咪	说,
A:	Mimi says,		

yǐ:	shuō	shén	me
乙:	说	什	么？
B:	Says what?		

jiǎ:	pāi	pāi	shǒu
甲:	拍	拍	手。
A:	Clap your hands.		

yǐ:	pāi	pāi	shǒu
乙:	拍	拍	手。
B:	Clap your hands.		

jiǎ:	mī	mī	shuō
甲:	咪	咪	说,
A:	Mimi says,		

yǐ:	shuō	shén	me
乙:	说	什	么？
B:	Says what?		

jiǎ:	shēn	shēn	shǒu
甲:	伸	伸	手。
A:	Put out your hands.		

yǐ:	shēn	shēn	shǒu
乙:	伸	伸	手。
B:	Put out your hands.		

jiǎ: mī mī shuō
甲: 咪 咪 说,
A: Mimi says,

yǐ: shuō shén me
乙: 说 什 么?
B: Says what?

jiǎ: pāi pāi tuǐ
甲: 拍 拍 腿。
A: Pat your legs.

yǐ: pāi pāi tuǐ
乙: 拍 拍 腿。
B: Pat your legs.

jiǎ: mī mī shuō
甲: 咪 咪 说,
A: Mimi says,

yǐ: shuō shén me
乙: 说 什 么?
B: Says what?

jiǎ: duò duò jiǎo
甲: 跺 跺 脚。
A: Stomp your feet.

yǐ: duò duò jiǎo
乙: 跺 跺 脚。
B: Stomp your feet.

jiǎ: mī mī shuō
甲: 咪 咪 说,
A: Mimi says,

yǐ:	shuō shén me
乙:	说 什 么？
B:	Says what?

jiǎ:	zhǐ zhǐ nǐ de shēn tǐ
甲:	指 指 你 的 身 体。
A:	Point to your body.

yǐ:	shēn tǐ
乙:	身 体。
B:	Body.

jiǎ:	mī mī shuō
甲:	咪 咪 说，
A:	Mimi says,

yǐ:	shuō shén me
乙:	说 什 么？
B:	Says what?

jiǎ:	shēn shēn nǐ de gē bo
甲:	伸 伸 你 的 胳 膊。
A:	Extend your arms.

yǐ:	gē bo
乙:	胳 膊。
B:	Arms.

jiǎ:	mī mī shuō
甲:	咪 咪 说，
A:	Mimi says,

yǐ:	shuō shén me
乙:	说 什 么？
B:	Says what?

	jiǎ	dà	shēng	shuō
甲:	大	声	说。	

A: Speak loudly.

	yǐ	dà	shēng	shuō
乙:	大	声	说。	

B: Speak loudly.

甲: 咪 咪 说， (jiǎ mī mī shuō)

A: Mimi says,

乙: 说 什 么？ (yǐ shuō shén me)

B: Says what?

甲: 小 声 点 儿。 (jiǎ xiǎo shēng diǎnr)

A: Speak quietly.

乙: 小 声 点 儿。 (yǐ xiǎo shēng diǎnr)

B: Speak quietly.

甲: 咪 咪 说， (jiǎ mī mī shuō)

A: Mimi says,

乙: 说 什 么？ (yǐ shuō shén me)

B: Says what?

甲: 站 起 来。 (jiǎ zhàn qǐ lái)

A: Stand up.

乙: 站起来。
yǐ zhàn qǐ lái
B: Stand up.

甲: 咪咪说，
jiǎ mī mī shuō
A: Mimi says,

乙: 说什么？
yǐ shuō shén me
B: Says what?

甲: 请坐下。
jiǎ qǐng zuò xià
A: Sit down, please.

乙: 请坐下。
yǐ qǐng zuò xià
B: Sit down, please.

甲: 咪咪说，
jiǎ mī mī shuō
A: Mimi says,

乙: 说什么？
yǐ shuō shén me
B: Says what?

甲: 谢谢你。
jiǎ xiè xie nǐ
A: Thank you.

THE END

教学参考

背景介绍

"形体带动说",简称"带动说"是James J Asher博士世界语教学方面的学说。"带动说"简言之就是通过动作学语言,用形体的动作来表达一个意思的同时说出这个词汇。"咪咪说"是根据这个学说在教汉语动词和名词上所做的一个尝试。如果要进一步探讨这个领域,需在www.tpr-world.com阅读有关这方面的文章。

教学建议

"咪咪说"要通过带动说教学生熟练掌握五官和四肢的中文词汇。教师在带动时要有所准备,话说得要有节奏,动作和词汇要贴切,要有一致性。学生同时从看、听和说三个渠道认知一个新词汇。带动说用得适当会使课堂气氛活跃,加速教学的效果。

教学步骤

一、老师指说五官和四肢的部位让学生听。
二、学生跟老师一起做带动说五官和四肢的词汇。
三、老师用"咪咪说"带动,学生用"说什么"呼应。
四、模范学生用"咪咪说"带动,其他学生用"说什么"呼应。
五、当学生熟悉"咪咪说"后,做类似"山姆说"的游戏。

教学评估

一、教师可以用其他词汇做"咪咪说"的游戏。
二、学生自己可以用"咪咪说"的内容做带动说的游戏。

请上网www.cheng-tsui.com查看作者有关TPR形体动作的建议。也请您与大家分享您的好主意和成果。

Teaching Reference

Background Information

"Mimi Says" uses a Total Physical Response (TPR) approach to teaching Chinese action verbs and concrete nouns. TPR was originated by Dr. James J. Asher of Cambridge University, England. Dr. Asher believes that TPR is a useful and powerful linguistic tool in foreign language teaching. For further information about TPR, visit www.tpr-world.com or read the book Learning Another Language through Actions by Dr. Asher.

Teaching Suggestions

"Mimi Says" will help students learn vocabulary through TPR actions. Students gather information through observing and hearing vocabulary in Chinese and then responding and speaking accordingly. Teachers must be well trained and prepared in order to use TPR effectively. The actions matching meanings should be clear and manageable for students to follow. Well designed and suitable Chinese vocabulary through TPR will bring increased student enthusiasm to the classroom.

Teaching Steps

Play the game of "Mimi Says" as one plays the game of "Simon Says."
1. The teacher points to parts of the body and names them while students observe and listen.
2. The teacher points to parts of the body and names them while students repeat.
3. The teacher gives "Mimi Says" directions and students respond.
4. A student gives "Mimi Says" directions and other students respond.

Assessment

1. Teachers can use other vocabulary to play the game "Mimi Says."
2. Students themselves can use vocabulary for parts of the body to play the game "Mimi Says."

Visit www.cheng-tsui.com for teaching suggestions from the author.
Also, share your own ideas and accomplishments!

Me

wǒ
我

zài mā ma yǎn jing lǐ wǒ shì nǚ ér / ér zi
在 妈 妈 眼 睛 里，我 是 女 儿 / 儿 子。
In my mother's eyes, I am a daughter/son.

zài bà ba yǎn jing lǐ wǒ shì nǚ ér / ér zi
在 爸 爸 眼 睛 里，我 是 女 儿 / 儿 子。
In my father's eyes, I am a daughter/son.

zài yé ye yǎn jing lǐ wǒ shì sūn nǚ / sūn zi
在 爷 爷 眼 睛 里，我 是 孙 女 / 孙 子。
In my grandpa's eyes on my father's side, I am a granddaughter/grandson.

zài nǎi nai yǎn jing lǐ wǒ shì sūn nǚ / sūn zi
在 奶 奶 眼 睛 里，我 是 孙 女 / 孙 子。
In my grandma's eyes on my father's side, I am a granddaughter/grandson.

zài gōng gong yǎn jing lǐ
在 公 公 眼 睛 里，
In my grandpa's eyes on my mother's side,

wǒ shì wài sūn nǔ　　wài sūn zi
我 是 外 孙 女／外 孙 子。
I am a granddaughter/grandson.

zài pó po yǎn jing lǐ
在 婆 婆 眼 睛 里，
In my grandma's eyes on my mother's side,

wǒ shì wài sūn nǔ　　wài sūn zi
我 是 外 孙 女／外 孙 子。
I am a granddaughter/grandson.

zài gē ge yǎn jing lǐ　wǒ shì dì di　mèi mei
在 哥 哥 眼 睛 里，我 是 弟 弟／妹 妹。
In my big brother's eyes, I am a younger brother/sister.

zài jiě jie yǎn jing lǐ　wǒ shì dì di　mèi mei
在 姐 姐 眼 睛 里，我 是 弟 弟／妹 妹。
In my big sister's eyes, I am a younger brother/sister.

zài dì di yǎn jing lǐ　wǒ shì gē ge　jiě jie
在 弟 弟 眼 睛 里，我 是 哥 哥／姐 姐。
In my younger brother's eyes, I am a big brother/sister.

zài mèi mei yǎn jing lǐ　wǒ shì gē ge　jiě jie
在 妹 妹 眼 睛 里，我 是 哥 哥／姐 姐。
In my younger sister's eyes, I am a big brother/sister.

zài lǎo shī yǎn jing lǐ　wǒ shì xué sheng
在 老 师 眼 睛 里，我 是 学 生。
In my teacher's eyes, I am a student.

zài péng you yǎn jing lǐ wǒ shì
在 朋 友 眼 睛 里，我 是 …

In my friend's eyes, I am…

zài　　　 yǎn jing lǐ wǒ shì péng you
在 … 眼 睛 里，我 是 朋 友。

In …'s eyes, I am a friend.

zài dà rén yǎn jing lǐ wǒ shì xiǎo hái zi
在 大 人 眼 睛 里，我 是 小 孩 子。

In an adult's eyes, I am a child.

zài dà xiàng yǎn jing lǐ wǒ shì xiǎo bù diǎnr
在 大 象 眼 睛 里，我 是 小 不 点 儿。

In an elephant's eyes, I am a little creature.

zài xiǎo mǎ yǐ yǎn jing lǐ wǒ shì jù rén
在 小 蚂 蚁 眼 睛 里，我 是 巨 人。

In an ant's eyes, I am a giant.

zài　　　 yǎn jing lǐ wǒ shì wài xīng rén
在 ET 眼 睛 里，我 是 外 星 人。

In ET's eyes, I am an alien.

zài wǒ de xiǎo gǒu yǎn jing lǐ wǒ shì zhǔ rén
在 我 的 小 狗 眼 睛 里，我 是 主 人。

In my dog's eyes, I am the master.

THE END

教学参考

背景介绍

对没有中国文化背景的学生来讲，中文的家庭亲属关系词汇较复杂。学起来有困惑。这里列出十八个以我为中心的句子，能深能浅，可加可减。学生可以根据自己不同的家庭背景，重新删减组织适合各自的内容，使学生从选择，阅读和背诵的过程中学习家庭成员的词汇并了解中国家庭成员的关系。

教学建议

一、教师和学生一起仔细阅读材料。
二、学生挑选与自己有关的内容。
三、学生重编自己的家庭成员关系的句子。
四、学生朗读和背诵自己的句子。
五、学生在班上背诵各自的句子并回答其他学生的问题。

评估小结

一、学生可以用中文正确说出自己的家庭成员。
二、学生可以用中文正确说出部分家庭亲属关系。

请上网 www.cheng-tsui.com 查看作者有关教学的建议。也请您与大家分享您的好主意和成果。

Teaching Reference

Background Information

"Me" consists of reading material designed to help students learn vocabulary pertaining to family members. It contains eighteen individual sentences detailing relationships among family members. In order to make the reading more enjoyable, a few non-family members are also included.

Teaching Suggestions

1. Teacher and students go over the reading material together.
2. Students choose the sentences that relate to them.
3. Students create some of their own sentences.
4. Students read and recite their own sentences.
5. Students answer their classmates' questions.

Assessment

1. Students are able to identify their family members by name in Chinese.
2. Students are able to describe some family relationships in Chinese.

Visit www.cheng-tsui.com for teaching suggestions from the author.
Also, share your own ideas and accomplishments!